ZEN
and the
SUTRAS

ZEN

and the

SUTRAS

➤ ◄

Albert Low

TUTTLE PUBLISHING
Boston • Rutland, Vermont • Tokyo

First published in 2000 by Tuttle Publishing, an imprint of Periplus Editions (HK) Ltd,
with editorial offices at 153 Milk Street, Boston, Massachusetts 02109.

Copyright © 2000 Albert Low

Library of Congress Cataloging-in-Publication Data

Low, Albert.
    Zen and the Sutras / by Albert Low. — 1st ed.
        p. cm.
    Includes bibliographical references.
    ISBN 0-8048-3201-3 (pb)
    1. Zen Buddhism—Sacred books. 2. Zen Buddhism—Doctrines.
    3. Tripitaka. Sutrapitaka—Criticism, interpretation, etc.
    I. Title.
    BQ9264.2.L68 2000
    294.3'85—dc21   98-53965
                                                        CIP

Distributed by

USA   JAPAN
Tuttle Publishing   Tuttle Shuppan
Distribution Center   RK Building, 2nd Floor
Airport Industrial Park   2-13-10 Shimo-Meguro, Meguro-Ku
364 Innovation Drive   Tokyo 153 0064
North Clarendon, VT 05759-9436   Tel: (03) 5437-0171
Tel: (802) 773-8930   Fax: (03) 5437-0755
Tel: (800) 526-2778

CANADA   SOUTHEAST ASIA
Raincoast Books   Berkeley Books Pte Ltd
8680 Cambie Street   5 Little Road #08-01
Vancouver, British Columbia   Singapore 536983
V6P 6M9   Tel: (65) 280-1330
Tel: (604) 323-7100   Fax: (65) 280-6290
Fax: (604) 323-2600

First edition
06 05 04 03 02 01 00   10 9 8 7 6 5 4 3 2 1

Design by Deborah Hodgdon

Printed in United States of America

CONTENTS

INTRODUCTION

This book will try to make accessible some of the sutras of Mahayana Buddhism and to show their value for spiritual practice. The sutras, whose name literally means "threads," are the records of the teachings of Buddha. They are intended for anyone who has an interest in spiritual practice, not simply for those who are practicing Zen Buddhism.

Origins of the Sutras

Buddhism was born with the teachings of Shakyamuni Buddha, who lived some 2,500 years ago. At about the beginning of the Common Era a revolution took place, and a new form of Buddhism, which has come to be known as Mahayana Buddhism, was born. This means that two kinds of sutras exist, the sutras of the earlier Buddhism—known as the Theravada, or teaching of the Elders—and the sutras of the Mahayana. The earlier sutras have been collected in what is called the Tripitika, or basket of writings, and form part of the Buddhist canon. These originally were written in Pali. The Mahayana sutras were written in Sanskrit, but unfortunately most are now preserved only in the Chinese or Tibetan translations.

When reading the sutras, one sometimes has the feeling that Buddha, or the masters, talked in a stiff and artificial way, whereas the opposite was quite likely true. Buddha was probably a very charismatic, down-to-earth man, capable of mixing freely with all kinds of people and of talking in the language of whoever was listening to him. It is the scholarly translations that can make Buddha's teaching seem tedious to those most interested in practice. Of course, we owe a great debt to the scholars who brought us this work, but for them, academic considerations often outweighed practical ones. Therefore, I shall change some of the wording to make the sutras more accessible.

The Sutras and Zen

Because this book is considering the sutras as manuals for practice, I shall be relating them to the koans used in Zen practice, which are based on the sutras. Koans are the sayings and doings of Buddha and of the Zen patriarchs and masters. The most famous of these is "The Sound of One Hand Clapping," introduced by Zen Master Hakuin. He said to his students, "You know the sound of two hands clapping. What is the sound of one hand clapping?" When one works with a koan, one must *demonstrate* one's insight into it to the Zen master. Explanations, theories, and speculations are of no use whatsoever. The purpose of the koan is to bring the student to awakening, which means to see into the truth that he or she is beyond all form. One is not a body, personality, soul, or spirit. One is certainly not nothing. Understanding, which is the integration of ideas and concepts around a core idea, serves the personality but is of little use in the resolution of koans.

I prefer to use the word *personality* rather than the word *ego* because *ego* has a negative feel about it. One could almost see the ego as the modern equivalent to the devil, whereas *personality* is a neutral word. It simply means the memories, judgments, prejudices, opinions, ideas, thoughts, and reactions that converge upon a core or center and make up what I call "me." Most of our time is spent one way or another in nurturing, protecting, developing, enhancing the personality. This is what is most precious to us. Our society encourages this absorption with the needs of the personality, and undertaking work that leads beyond the personality is looked upon as slightly weird. Zen is work of this kind; it has nothing of value for the personality.

Is Zen Anti-intellectual?

Zen has a reputation for being anti-intellectual. This is undoubtedly due in part to the fact that the masters constantly reject their students' speculations and theories. But it is also due to the fact that Zen came fully into its own in the West at the same time that "New Age" thinking was blossoming and it was fashionable to criticize the "establishment," including academic studies. This anti-intellectualism comes also from a general despair at the bankruptcy of much that passes for traditional religion. Many believe that religious thinking has been locked into meaningless phrases and dead dogma.

Such people are relieved to hear about a Zen master who, when asked by his student to tell him about the principles of Buddhism, turned on him and snapped, "No barking like a dog!" They would no doubt agree with the monk who, when the master asked what parts of the Buddhist scriptures had been written by the devil, retorted, "All of them!" The master received this answer with great hoots of laughter and congratulated the monk by saying, "No one will be able to take the rise out of you!"

Ironically, in the sutras that follow we will read again and again that words cannot get us to the truth. For example, Ananda, the cousin of Buddha, was his disciple and close attendant. Ananda was so noted for his intellectual ability that the early sutras are said to be the result of his having remembered, word for word, every-thing Buddha said and after Buddha's death recalling the talks so they could be transcribed. Nevertheless, during Buddha's lifetime Ananda was unable to come to awakening, and it was said that this inability was caused by his intellectual capacity. In the *Surangama Sutra*, Ananda says, "Although I have become the disciple of Bud-dha, my heart is not yet absorbed in Awakening. I am like a prodi-gal son who has forsaken his father. I now see that, in spite of my learning, if I am not able to put it into practice, I am no better than an unlearned man. It is like a man talking about food, but who never eats and so does not become satisfied. We are all entangled in these two hindrances: knowledge and learning, and vexation and suffering."[1]

While it is true that we are entangled this way, we must be careful how we interpret such a saying. It is evident that the mas-ters were well versed in the sutras. Zen Master Tokusan, for exam-ple, knew the *Diamond Sutra* well and, before meeting with his own Zen master, lectured upon it extensively; the founder of the Zen sect, Bodhidharma, the very one who preached self-realization outside the scriptures, nevertheless advocated the *Lankavatara Sutra*; Zen Master Hogen knew the *Avatamsaka Sutra* well, and koan twenty-six in the *Mumonkan*, in which Hogen is involved, comes out of the teaching of that sutra. Other koans, too, make reference directly or indirectly to the sutras. The auto-biography of yet another Zen master, Hui Neng, subsequently became the *Platform Sutra*, one of the sutras so condemned by those who rejected intellectual and sutra studies.

This apparent distaste for the intellect was not shared by all Korean Zen masters. Much of the Korean Zen Buddhist tradition goes back to Zen Master Chinul, who came to awakening while reading the *Platform Sutra*. Later, he meditated deeply on the place that the sutras have in Zen training and came to the conclu-sion that "what the World Honored One said with his mouth are the teachings. What the patriarchs transmitted with their minds is

Zen. The mouth of the Buddha and the minds of the patriarchs can certainly not be contradictory. How can [students of both Zen and the scholastic schools] not plumb the fundamental source but instead, complacent in their own training, wrongly foment disputes and waste their time?"[2]

Therefore, as we read the sutras, let us bear in mind this injunction of Rinzai: "I do not care whether you are well versed in the Sutras, I only care whether you have true and genuine insight."

1. *The Buddhist Bible*, edited by Dwight Goddard (Boston: Beacon Press, 1966), p. 127.
2. *The Collected Works of Chinul*, translated by Robert E. Buswell, Jr. (Honolulu: University of Hawaii Press, 1983).

CHAPTER 1

THE KOANS AND THE SUTRAS

*A monk asked Zen Master Joshu, "Does a dog
have the Buddha-nature?" Joshu replied, "Mu!"*
MUMONKAN

Buddha said his teaching is like a raft, to be used simply as a means of crossing the ocean of birth and death. On one occasion he asked, "And when you are across, will you continue to carry the raft on your head?" This is what we have done. Not only have we carried the raft on our head, but we have also put it into a glass case in a museum. We have studied, analyzed, and reproduced it; we have asked, Who really made it? What is it made of? How was it made? When was it made? What kind of wood was used? Far from using the teaching to cross the ocean and then letting it go, we have even brought it into the living room and tried to find a place for it among the furniture.

Some say that Buddha's way is a science, that we should accept his teaching as a theory and then prove it for ourselves. Much can be said for this point of view, but it still implies that something needs to be known, learned, discovered, or uncovered; it still suggests that what is a theory will later become fact. Yet one should not look in the realm of fact, in the realm of ontology or epistemology, or even ethics or theology, for the meaning of what Buddha taught.

When Buddha said his teaching was a raft, he meant that it was directed toward practice. He was not interested in philosophy or theology, even though so many philosophies have been founded in his name and even though his teaching has been made into a religion. It has been claimed at different times that his teaching was idealist, realist, pessimistic, otherworldly. But none of these labels apply to Buddha's teaching because, as he said, when one reaches the other shore, one discards it. A theory claims an absolute status for itself—it claims to be true, and true not only for the time being, but also for all time. But it could be said that Buddha was not even interested in the truth, at least not in the truth that can be expressed in concepts and ideas, that can be debated.

Perhaps the nearest we can get to a correct designation of Buddha's teaching is to call it *soteriology*. Unfortunately, this word has strong Christian overtones, but when we remember that it is derived from the Greek *soterion*, meaning "deliverance," its aptness is obvious. One should accept the teaching as a way of deliverance, and this would imply deliverance from the teaching, as well.

The Importance of the Sutras

Scholars have preserved the raft, and for this we must be very grateful. Buddha did not say that we had to swim across the ocean of birth and death, which is what so many self-styled teachers mean when they declare that no teaching is necessary and that religions simply cause conflict and confusion. Thanks to the work of the scholars, those of us who want to get to the other shore have the teaching available and in a form that is more or less accessible. But to benefit from it, to be "delivered" by it, we must take it out of the realm of scholarship into the realm of practice. To do this we must make it seaworthy. We must throw off much of the ballast, get rid of what is not necessary, and make it more serviceable, and it is to further this goal that this book was written.

The Zen masters undoubtedly studied the sutras, and many of

the koans, those enigmatic stories used in practice, come directly out of this study. They used the sutras as tools for work, not as objects for appreciation. Let us try to do the same. We shall be studying the *Prajnaparamita Hridaya*, the *Diamond Sutra*, parts of the *Vimalakirti Sutra*, the *Lankavatara Sutra* and the *Surangama Sutra*. The first two are sufficiently short that we can consider them in their entirety; the others are much longer. The first three are all from the Prajnaparamita School. The *Lankavatara Sutra* is the sutra most closely associated with the entry of Zen into China; Bodhidharma, the first Chinese patriarch, brought it with him from India to China in the fifth century C.E. The last, the *Surangama Sutra* is said to be the key sutra, because when it is no longer taught or studied Buddha's teaching will cease to exist.

A Few Words on Metaphysics and Ontology

Before going on with our study of the sutras, let us place them, and Buddhism in general, within the scheme of human spirituality. In the evolution of consciousness and culture, two forms of religious expression have emerged: *prayer* and *meditation*. Whether we pray or meditate depends upon our basic metaphysics, specifically our basic *ontology*. Just as one of Molière's characters was surprised to find that he spoke and wrote prose, so most of us are surprised to learn that we have a basic metaphysics and ontology. Nevertheless, as young children, all of us come to some conclusions about the world and its structure, as well as our place within this structure. Philosophy, or at least metaphysics, could be looked upon as the way we reach these conclusions and the conclusions themselves. Most of us gain, and hold, our philosophy unconsciously, so it remains unexamined.

Most of us, moreover, opt for some dualistic understanding of the world and our place in it. Why this is so is out of the range of this discussion;[1] let me just say that we most often decide the *world* is "out there" and *I* am "in here." Because most people do not think about it any further, this view becomes entrenched as their reality and is taken for granted. So instead of saying, "It is *as though* a world is out there, and *as though* I am in here," we say, and believe without doubt, "It is there, and I am here."

Even so, we have an intuitive sense of our own individuality and the world as coherent, an undivided whole. Do we not speak of a *universe*, which means "turning toward the one?" This intuition comes from a deep sense of unity. Yet, although on the one hand we have the intuition of a fundamental unity, on the other we experience dualistically: "me" and "the world." Our dualistic view of the world, according to Buddha, gives birth to suffering. The very word Buddha used for suffering was *dukkha*, which means "duality" or "twoness" (*du* = two; *kha* = ness). To cure this suffering we have to heal the wound we have created by our way of viewing the world. The word *heal* comes from the same verbal root as *whole* and *holy*.

We are impelled to find wholeness again, and most of us believe that we must do so by looking either "out there" or "in here." When we look for unity out there, in a religious way, we seek a transcendent One or Whole. Traditionally, in Christianity this One has been called God. Alternatively, when we look for unity "in here," we look for it as a transcendent Whole, but this time as a unified Self or supreme, subjective One such as Atman in the Vedanta tradition. This is often called the Self with a capital *S* to distinguish it from the dualistic self of everyday experience. Prayer could be looked upon as an attempt to make contact with the transcendent One "out there" and meditation as an attempt to make contact with the transcendent One "in here."

Of course, this is an oversimplification of thoughts and perceptions that can be extremely complex and subtle. Furthermore, not everyone takes their original metaphysics as an ultimate statement of truth, and many have subjected this metaphysics to subtle analysis. Even so, "God" and the "Self" are the two broad ways that human beings have gone in search of peace and relief from suffering. If we see Unity as objective, as out there, then the subjective, the Self, is but a ghost or phantom. In this case, God, Brahman, or Allah is the Supreme Reality or Supreme Being. If unity is "in here," subjective, then the objective is an illusion, the world is a dream. In this case the Self is the Supreme Reality.

Most people believe that Buddhism opts for the second of these alternatives. This belief, although erroneous, is not confined simply to non-Buddhists, but is also held by some Buddhists, including many Zen Buddhists who believe that the Buddhist, while meditating, searches for transcendental unity through the Self or Subjective Unity (sometimes known as Buddha nature, or Self-Nature). Other Buddhists have come to believe that Unity is out there in a Pure Land attained by way of the Amida Buddha. This, too, is erroneous—Buddhism is based upon neither subjective Unity nor objective Unity, nor upon a fusion of the two, nor even upon a denial of the importance of Unity. When Joshu replied, "Mu!" or "No!" to the monk, he was saying no to a transcendent One, both as object and as subject.

Impermanence, Suffering, and No Absolute Self

The basis of Buddhism is *impermanence, suffering*, and *no absolute self*. The *Anguttara-Nikaya Sutra* says that it is "an unalterable fact, an unalterable condition of existence and an eternal law that all karmic formations are impermanent (*anicca*) . . . subject to suffering (*dukkha*) . . . and non-absolute (*anatman*, i.e., without unchangeable or absolute ego-identity)."

The sutra is saying that no world exists "out there." What we conceive of as a fixed, permanent, and absolute "something" is an illusion. It would naturally follow that no Supreme Being, no fixed cause uncaused, in fact, no fixed and permanent God can be found. God, too, is impermanent. It would also follow that no self, no soul or Spirit, no Overself, Cosmic Consciousness, or Buddha nature—in other words, no ultimate Subjective One—lurks "in here." Buddha nature, too, as Dogen said, is impermanence. *Anatman* means just that: no self. Furthermore, it is the very belief in an objective One or a subjective One that is the cause of suffering.

On the face of it, it would seem that Buddha was nihilistic, that he was preaching a doctrine of total negation. But those who think this way have yet to see how radical Buddha's teaching was. To appreciate this, let us consider negation as a way.

Negation has been a way by which mystics have attempted to express transcendental unity. For example, in the Christian tradition two main streams can be found: the kataphatic and the apophatic. The *kataphatic* tradition is "the tradition of light; it arrives at an understanding of God through affirmation: we come to know God by affirming he possesses all the perfection we find in creatures."[2] Thomas Merton felt that this tradition penetrates to the deepest essence. By contrast, the *apophatic* tradition, he felt, "concerns itself with the most fundamental datum of all faith—and one that is often forgotten: the God who reveals Himself to us in His Word has revealed Himself as unknown in His ultimate essence. The presence of God shining, not in clear vision, but as 'unknown.'"[3]

God as referred to here is a God of extreme subtlety. God *is*, but is unknown. God's being is absolute, but absolutely unknowable. Absolute transcendental Unity is affirmed, but as unknowable.

The Buddha's Way

The Buddha's Way is the way of neither affirmation nor denial, kataphatic nor apophatic. In a well-known koan, a Zen master, holding up a stick, says, "If you call this a stick you conceal it; if you say it is not a stick you deny it. What is it?" Some commentators feel that the master, by his words and actions, simply wants to help us escape from the snare of language. Yet, although language does represent a snare for the unwary, it would be a mistake to think that this koan is simply pointing to a problem of words and thoughts and that the master is just wanting to get us beyond them. This would be like saying that Buddhism and Zen are simply other expressions of the apophatic tradition. Certainly, *stick* is a word, so to say "it" is a stick is to say that "it" can be known; to say "it" is not a stick is to say that "it" cannot be known.[4] Either way, we are still left with "it." To say it is a stick is to affirm; this is in the kataphatic tradition. To say it is not a stick is to negate, and this is in the apophatic tradition.

In another koan, a Zen master said, "If you say you have a stick I will give you one, if you say you do not have a stick I will take it from you." In other words, when you say you have a stick you are simply grasping an *idea*, so the stick can still be given to you. If, on the other hand, you say you do not have a stick, you may have gotten beyond the idea, but you are still left with an underlying, inarticulate "something": an ontological residue that can be taken away. To say you have a stick is in the kataphatic tradition. To say you do not have a stick is in the apophatic tradition. How does one get beyond both? The sutras that we shall be discussing, as well as Zen koans, are responses to this question.

The Sutras and Awakening

Zen Master Bassui had this to say about sutras:

> If you truly want to read the sutras, you first have to awaken the mind that does the reading. All formal readings from the sutras are ultimately destructive. The wonderful dharma of one's mind does not change through successive eons; it is the essence of all sutras. . . . When you see the wordless sutra only once, the sutras of all the heavens, with their golden words which fill one's eyes, are clearly manifest. If you read the sutras with this kind of understanding, you will never be idle throughout endless eons. If you do not have this kind of understanding you will spend your whole life covering the surface of black beans [words].[5]

The basic message of all the Mahayana sutras is awakening, what Bassui calls here "see[ing] the wordless sutra." It is, of course, entirely possible to come to awakening without ever having heard of the sutras, Buddha, or even awakening itself. In one of the more celebrated accounts of awakening, Zen Master Hui Neng came to awakening when hearing a monk recite from the *Diamond Sutra*. Up until that time he had not heard of either Buddhism or awakening. Throughout the history of the human race, untold numbers of people must have come to this kind of spontaneous awakening without the aid of the scriptures.

Although it is true that some people make a fortune by winning a lottery, most of us have to work for our living. Just as it would be foolish to sit and wait for pennies to fall from heaven, it would be foolish to sit and wait for awakening to strike. Just as we have to work for our physical well-being, we have to work for our spiritual well-being. It is for this kind of work that the sutras become important.

The intellectual mind is of limited value on the spiritual path, but it must be satisfied if we are to commit ourselves fully to the work. Although the mind eventually must understand that it is unable to settle the great questions that, at some level, haunt us throughout our lives, a certain amount of preparatory work must be done, and reading and studying can help with this preparation. Reading can also help us understand that true spiritual work is so difficult because it has nothing to offer the personality. One certainly can practice Zen to enhance health and psychological well-being, to develop natural concentration, or to improve creativity; this is what Yasutani roshi would have called Bompu Zen. Nevertheless, true spiritual practice, the practice that leads beyond form, beyond thought and idea, beyond the sense of self, is not done to yield these kinds of results.

Spiritual practice is, from the point of view of the personality, useless, but then so is listening to music, or being at peace with someone you love, or even living. One of the diseases of our age is the belief that everything must have a use. The theory of evolution, which has now taken on all the characteristics of a religious dogma, preaches the dreary and narrow-minded belief that all of life—all its beauty, complexity, and intricacy, all of it—serves simply for the transmission of genes. It would say that all life's activity is yoked to survival. It seems that, with the theory of evolution, consequence is often confused with cause.

The meaning of existence is "no-meaning," which is not the same as absence of meaning. The expression *no-meaning* points to a meaning that cannot be grasped in terms of utility. This no-meaning is intrinsic in all spiritual endeavors.

Although the personality needs meaning that can be defined, understood, grasped, it is possible for meaning to lie beyond "use-fulness." But to truly appreciate this requires awakening. Reading and study can introduce the mind to this possibility; they can provide the kind of background that eventually enables the critical, discriminating mind to be suspended for a while so that a deeper and more penetrating awareness can be aroused.

Meditation and the Sutras

There are three aspects to Zen practice: meditation, concentration, and contemplation. *Zazen*, which is often called Zen meditation, includes all three, but the emphasis in Zen practice is upon contemplation, what is also known as being "one with." Contemplation of the breath, for example, means to be one with the breath. It is not a way of controlling the breath, nor a way of observing, visualizing, or "watching" the breath. Contemplation is far more flexible than concentration; it is what has been called *wu-wei*, or the doing of no-doing. In Zen it is also called *shikantaza*.

Concentration, nevertheless, is also often necessary, particularly when working on a first koan. However, meditation is also of great value. I have spoken about these three aspects of Zen practice in other books,[6] but let me briefly review them here.

Concentration means "with a center." It requires great energy and is a way of focusing the mind to enable it to become rooted. If when sitting in zazen the back is straight and the center of gravity low, then this energy, called *joriki* in Zen, enables the mind to become steadfast and not troubled by random thoughts. With this steadfastness, this concentration, it becomes possible for contemplation to take over.

Many years of hard practice are required before contemplation in its purest form becomes possible, and one must pass through a long period during which neither concentration nor contemplation alone, but instead an amalgam of the two is used. This often involves long and very dry periods during which practice seems pointless and without reward. I have heard these periods likened to crossing the great Gobi Desert. One must have great faith to go on, and at the very time when it is needed most, we so often do not have this kind of faith. It is for this reason that meditation is so necessary.

Meditation is the process of taking an idea and allowing thoughts to circle around it. The mind is kept flexible but taut. Without the tautness one cannot hold the meditation idea. As a basis for meditation I recommend using sayings of masters of various spiritual traditions, including, of course, Zen Buddhism: masters such as Nisargadatta Maharaj, Ramana Maharshi, Ramakrishna, St. John of the Cross, the anonymous author of *The Cloud of Unknowing*, the Desert Fathers, the Bhagavad Gita, St. Julian of Norwich, St. Teresa of Avila, St. Thérèse of Lisieux, and so on. One reads just a little, a few phrases only, then allows what has been read to sink into the mind. One makes no effort to understand, but allows the mind to come to its own understanding.

One should not do this to saiety; in other words, one must stop well before the mind starts to want to grasp what is being read. Normally, about twenty minutes is all that is necessary. One way the meditative process can be prolonged is by meditating while doing some handwork, such as knitting, rug hooking, embroidery, or some other simple, repetitive task. One reads a few sentences, then allows the meaning to soak into the mind while doing some of the handwork. One then reads a little more, and so on. This meditative practice is like rain falling on the desert. It awakens faith and gives encouragement to continue, even though one must work mostly in the dark and without clear direction through the vast desert of the mind. The Desert Fathers used this kind of meditative practice. They would weave baskets while meditating, and when a basket was finished they would undo it and start again.

I wrote this book with meditation in mind because truly pondering the sutras is itself a valuable meditation practice. The sutras provide a background for general practice and, later on, for koan practice. They help to point up the limitations of the mind (indeed, this is a constant theme of the sutras), so the discriminating mind will be more ready to let go and allow deeper parts of the mind to take over.

The Sutras and Practice

I have tried to approach the sutras from the point of view of practice. This may mean that I sometimes wander away from the literal meaning. However, my interpretation comes from years of intense practice, many of these spent working on koans. When working on the text of a sutra, I come as I would to a koan. The first, or preliminary, koan is often called a breakthrough koan— breaking through or awakening to the truth that one is beyond all form. In subsequent koan practice one must work by way of the original awakening to "see into" the koan in question. The resolution of each koan is a new awakening, so the original awakening is broadened and integrated more securely into everyday life. Awakening is not a single, homogenous event, but, like a diamond, has many facets. Subsequent koan practice enables one to penetrate this vast treasure house. But such work only is possible within the light of the original awakening.

Working with the sutras and working with the koans are not different, and ideally both kinds of work should come out of the original awakening. As Bassui said above, "If you truly want to read the sutras, you first have to awaken the mind that does the reading. All formal readings from the sutras are ultimately destructive." Being able to respond to all the questions a teacher poses about a koan is not the same as seeing into it, and confusing the two can keep one forever blocked, unable to gain access to the pearl of great price. To see into a koan as well as into a sutra, you must first awaken the mind that does the seeing into. To awaken is to arouse primordial, nonreflected knowing; such knowing always is sudden and penetrating. It cannot be unconscious, nor can one person bestow awakening upon another. The value of a teacher is to differentiate pure gold from fool's gold. One needs someone who is able to recognize fool's gold as spurious and help one to reject it; but pure gold one knows.

On the face of it, it might seem that only a few people would be able to read the sutras, and if by reading the sutras we mean penetrating deeply into their meaning, this, alas, is true. However, this does not mean that others cannot benefit from them. All of us, intrinsically, are awakened. When we read something and are struck by its truth, moved by the simple beauty and rightness of what it says, we feel that this brilliance comes from what we are reading. But it does not. It is like the dew on the grass on an early summer's day. Scintillating like a million gems, the dew flashes in the morning sunlight. But this brilliance and sparkle all comes from the sunlight. In the same way, the brilliance and truth that seem to shine out of the words of the masters is nothing other than the reflection of your own light, the brilliance of your own awakened nature.

This is the basis of meditation: dwelling in that brilliance, dwelling in it but not trying to grasp or understand it. These flashes may not come very often at first, but when they do one must be prepared. It is like what Jesus said to the foolish virgins: "Watch, for you know not the day nor the hour." This watchfulness, this nonabiding in the meaning, allows the shaft of one's own sunlight to lighten the darkness; it is the fruit of one's faith, but it is also a way by which faith is deepened and strengthened. However, without a solid practice involving concentration and contemplation, without long stretches in the Gobi Desert in the authentic quest to go beyond the dictates and needs of the personality, this meditative practice can easily fall into a form of sentimentality. Oscar Wilde said that sentimentality is enjoying an emotion for which one has not paid the price, and surely the spiritual way is flooded with sentimentality. Therefore, although I shall try to rescue the sutras from being just objects of intellectual study, I cannot make them easier to read.

Because all the sutras pass over the same terrain but from different directions, you will find considerable overlap and repetition. I have tried to allow each sutra to speak with its own inflections and accents; this, too, may increase the duplication. However, this is not necessarily a drawback. We do not read the sutras for information or to increase our store of knowledge any more than we listen to the lyrics of music for intellectual reasons. In both cases, repetition may enhance, rather than detract from, interest and value. Furthermore, because I have dealt with each sutra on its own, and not from the point of view of any overarching theory, you may read the following chapters in any order. Chapter 6, on the *Lankavatara Sutra*, may be a little tough for some people, and, if this is the case for you, skip it and come back to it later

I have included a brief bibliography of the sutras, and some books that discuss them. I have put in bold letters the titles of those books that were primary sources as I was writing this book. The others I read to help clarify difficulties arising from translation. I have kept footnotes to a minimum because, as I have said, this book is primarily for those who wish to practice.

1. For more on this topic see my books *The Iron Cow of Zen* (1991) and *The Butterfly's Dream* (1993), both published by Charles E. Tuttle.

2. William H. Shannon, *Thomas Merton's Dark Path* (New York: Penguin Books, 1982), p. 9.

3. Ibid., p. 10.

4. To talk about "it" shows what is meant by the snare of language, and why masters use koans to circumvent this problem.

5. *Mud and Water: A Collection of Talks by the Zen Master Bassui*, translated by Arthur Braverman (San Francisco: North Point Press, 1989), p. 60.

6. See, for example, *An Invitation to Practice Zen* (Rutland, VT: Charles E. Tuttle, 1989).

Chapter 2

THE PRAJNAPARAMITA
TRADITION

To slice through Buddhas, Patriarchs
I grip my polished sword
One glance at my mastery
Emptiness bites the dust

Written on awakening

From the beginning not a thing is. This is the fundamental theme
of the Prajnaparamita sutras, and in this chapter I shall discuss
what this statement means in preparation for our examination of
the sutras. In particular, we shall consider the notion of a Supreme
Being, or an underlying being, a substratum, which is so important
to many religious beliefs but which the Prajnaparamita tradition
sees as illusory.

Prajna

The first three sutras we will be discussing are from the Prajnaparamita tradition. Let us first take this word apart and understand
what it means. As we have seen, the sutras and the koans are the
sayings or, sometimes, the doings of Buddha and the Zen patriarchs. They come, in other words, from an "awakened mind." To
realize what a master says, we must be one with the awakened
mind, or, more simply, we must be awakened. The awakened mind
is no other than prajna. A sutra is the full expression of prajna, and
seeing into a koan is also the full expression of prajna. The *Diamond*

21

Sutra says, "Arouse the mind without resting it upon anything." This saying helps us to get a handle on the word *prajna*.

The word *prajna* consists of a prefix, *pra-*, and a root word *-jna*, which means "primordial knowing." Prajna, according to Herbert Guenther and Chogyam Trungpa,[1] is an intensification of the "cognitive processes." Unfortunately, the expression "cognitive processes" suggests something special, philosophical, abstract; perhaps a better word would be *knowing*. "Knowing" is more concrete, immediate. Whereas we are confident everyone knows, we cannot help feeling that only special people would have "cognitive processes." In this case prajna would mean an "aroused," or awakened knowing, knowing that has been released from all the extraneous material that has been accumulated.

Again, to read the sutras and to work with koans we must arouse the mind without resting upon anything. A koan is not a nonsense statement designed to throw sand into the intellectual works, nor is it a riddle. "Why did the chicken cross the road?" is a riddle. It is not nonsense because it has an answer: "Because it wanted to get to the other side." A riddle calls for a response at the same level as the question. A koan calls for a leap to a new level.

Paramitas

Now, let us talk for a moment about the paramitas, so that we may understand what *Prajnaparamita* means. Tradition speaks of six paramitas, that is, the six virtues or requirements for spiritual practice. The word *paramita* means literally "that which has reached the other shore." Thus, for example, *Prajnaparamita* refers to reaching the other shore by way of prajna. The six paramitas are these: (1) *Dána* means generosity or giving, in both the material and the spiritual sense. Dána implies compassion and the willingness to give of oneself as well as the willingness to give material goods. (2) *Shila* means discipline and the eradication of all passions. (3) *Kshanti* means patience and tolerance.

(4) *Víraya*, or exertion, refers to a one-pointed attitude toward practice. (5) *Dhyána* can mean meditation, but it can also mean samadhi, or beyond the opposites of subject and object. And, finally, (6) *prajna* means the attainment of wisdom.

What is important from our point of view is that, according to the Prajnaparamita School, while all the virtues are essential for the spiritual life, they nevertheless are founded upon the virtue of wisdom or prajna.[2]

The Prajnaparamita School

Traditionally, as I mentioned earlier, it is said that Ananda, Buddha's cousin and close disciple, dictated the sutras, that he had such a good memory that he was able to remember word for word all that Buddha said during his lifetime. However, the Mahayana sutras appeared long after Ananda died, so, obviously, Buddha could not have given them during his lifetime. It is not known who wrote the *Prajnaparamita Sutras*. According to Edward Conze, the renowned Buddhist scholar, the first formulation of the doctrine occurred in about 100 B.C.E., in a work with the imposing title *Ratnagunasamcayagáthá*. This work introduced the terms *bodhisattva* and *mahasattva*. Further, it gave a new "goal" of practice. It was no longer enough simply to escape from the wheel of birth and death; one now had to achieve full Buddhahood.

Prajna came into its own also in this text as the "mother of all Buddhas." In the eightfold path of the Buddha, which formed a part of the four noble truths of early Buddhism, prajna was not mentioned. The last step of the eightfold path was dhyana, or samadhi. Moving prajna to center stage was, as we shall see, a major change.

One of the revolutions of the Prajnaparamita School was the replacement of the goal of the arhat with the goal of the bodhisattva. The *arhat* was one who, through long cycles of existence, had so perfected himself that he was on earth for the last time. At the end of his current life he would reach blessed rest. Buddhists often referred to this as "getting off the wheel of birth and death." This was not the aim of the bodhisattva, of whom the *Ratnagunasamcayagáthá* says:

> *Just so the Bodhisattva,*
> *when he comprehends the dharmas as he should,*
> *Does not retire into Blessed rest.*
> *In prajna then he dwells.*

Blessed rest, *nirvriti* in Sanskrit, is the Nirvana that excludes the world of suffering. The new teaching declares that salvation is to be found not in escape from, but in the midst of the difficulties of the world. One is reminded of the koan in which Zen Master Joshu, when still a novice, asks Nansen, "What is the Way?" And Nansen replies, "Everyday mind is the Way." It is this understanding that is so important in the practice of Zen, as we shall see when we come to the *Vilmalakirti Sutra*, which extols the virtues of ordinary, everyday mind and, therefore, of lay practice.

When Hakuin says in his verse *In Praise of Zazen*, "True self is no self, our own self is no Self," he is giving the essence of the teaching, a teaching that Buddha summed up in one word, *anatman*. This same teaching is emphasized several times in the *Diamond Sutra*, —for example, when it says, "No Bodhisattva who is a real Bodhisattva cherishes the idea of an ego-entity, a personality, a being, or a separated individual."

Furthermore, this teaching of Prajnaparamita, instead of saying that one should be detached from worldly possessions and ties, insists that all worldly ties are *empty*, and in no aspect of existence is there a place to rest. In other words, no attachment is possible because ultimately no thing exists to which one can be attached. This is *anicca*, the other basic teaching of Buddha. The ultimate unreality of "being," whether "out there" or "in here," is emphasized in the *Ratnagunasamcayagáthá* when it is said:

If for eons countless as the sands of the Ganges
The Leader himself would continue to pronounce
  the word "being,"
Still, pure from the very start, no being could ever
  result from his speaking.

In the *Ratnagunasamcayagátha*, and subsequently in the Prajnaparamita, a further step yet was envisaged, and that was to
affirm that not even any transcendental wisdom could be attained:

No wisdom can we get hold of, no highest perfection.
No Bodhisattva, no thought of enlightenment whatever.

If there is no wisdom, no highest perfection, no Bodhisattva,
what is there?

No wonder, then, that the sutra says:

When told of this, if not bewildered and in no way anxious
A Bodhisattva courses in the Well Gone's wisdom.

Mahayana or Hinayana?

Traditionally, the development of Buddhism has been divided into
two phases. The first phase, which predominated until the beginning of the Common Era, was known as *Theravada*, or *Hinayana*.[3]
The second phase, which began with the Prajnaparamita School,
was known as *Mahayana*. According to the teaching of the
Hinayana, samadhi was the ultimate goal. *Samadhi* literally means
"to stand firm" and refers to an advanced state of contemplation in
which it is possible for the aspirant to step off the wheel of birth
and death and enter into blessed rest, Nirvana, the extinction of
desire. For the mahayanist, simply attaining salvation for oneself is
not enough; one must attain awakening for all sentient beings.

When Buddha left home and journeyed through the forest, he
met several teachers, each of whom taught him an increasingly
subtle form of samadhi. It is said that Buddha became proficient

in all these teachings but refused to accept any of them as the ultimate way to salvation. Instead, he continued with his search, suffered through years of ascetic practice, and finally, while practicing zazen under the Bo tree, came to deep awakening. It was with this awakening that Buddha became satisfied his journey was at an end.

Awakening or Samadhi?

The debate between awakening and samadhi does not concern Buddhism alone; it pervades the spiritual endeavor of all humankind. The debate can be expressed by this question: Is the ultimate in spiritual work a return to an eternal substratum of peace, an all-pervading consciousness by which the whole universe is sustained, or is it necessary to go beyond even this substratum? For example, Taoism, which contributed much to the development of Zen Buddhism, subscribed to this incipient substratum.

Tao-hsin, the fourth Zen patriarch, quoted Chu'ang-Tzu as saying that heaven and earth are one finger. "But," Tao-hsin went on,

> According to the Sutra of the Word of the Law, Buddhists do not look upon one as one, because they wish to break with the relativity of number; it is the man of lesser intelligence who considers one as one. This is why I say that Chu'ang-Tzu still had a mind obstructed by the notion of one. Lao Tzu says that in the profound mystery lies a subtle spirit. This is because he keeps to the idea of an inner mind, even though he has let go of an outside. *The Avatamsaka Sutra* says, one must not be attached to duality, there is neither one nor two. *The Vimalakirti Sutra* says mind is neither on the inside nor on the outside nor between the two, it is our Intuition. Therefore I say that Lao Tsu stagnates in the mind and in consciousness.

Another old master pointed out the practical consequences of holding to an underlying being when he criticized the Confucianists and the Taoists for maintaining a substratum of consciousness and serenity. He said that many sages wander astray by holding on to serene tranquillity in themselves. "In my opinion," this master went on, "it is by maintaining tranquillity that the Confucianists of the Sung dynasty became attached to the state of mind which did not allow any feeling of joy, anger, sadness, or pleasure to arise. It is just by maintaining tranquillity that Lao Tzu insists that one finally arrives at nothing and so comes to tranquillity and serenity. The concentrated state at which the Arhats and Hinayanists arrive, as well as the fruit of their illumination, are also simply due to keeping to a state of tranquillity, and to that alone."

Different religions have given different names to this substratum: God, Buddha, the Self, cosmic consciousness, the Higher Self, Atman, and, in Zen Buddhism, Buddha nature, and so on. Generally speaking, Vedanta, early Buddhism, and the Pure Land School of Mahayana subscribe to the idea of this substratum, and it also pervades much of the Soto teaching of Zen. In the Christian tradition, the poems of St. John of the Cross extol the virtues of what I am calling samadhi. However, Buddha, as I have just pointed out, underwent intense suffering rather than accept samadhi as the ultimate.

The difference between the two approaches is well summed up in two poems that appear early in the *Platform Sutra* of Hui Neng. One of them was written by the head monk of a monastery, the other by Hui Neng, who was resident at that monastery. The poems were written at the request of the abbot, the Fifth Patriarch. He declared that whoever wrote the poem reflecting the deepest attainment would succeed him.

The head monk wrote:

The body is the Bodhi tree,
The mind is like a clear mirror,
At all times we must strive to polish it
And let no dust alight.

Many of us think like this: If only I could keep the mind pure and serene, everything would be OK. The dust is the dust of thought and opinion, concept and idea, all that rambling confusion that passes through our heads throughout the day. The head monk is saying that a mind, as a substratum, underlies all that we do, and spiritual practice is keeping this mind free from dust. The mind would then be like a mirror, reflecting all without distinction. When Hui-Neng read the verse, he realized that the head monk had not yet seen into the complete truth, so he also wrote a verse:

Bodhi originally has no tree,
The mirror also has no stand.
From the beginning not a thing is
Where is there room for dust?

Hui-Neng is saying that even a mirror, whether covered by dust or not, is still *something*, and is therefore itself but dust. Another teacher said much the same thing as Hui-Neng's third line in different words: "Emptiness itself is empty."

The head monk's verse is said to be typical of the Northern School of Buddhism in Zen, while Hui Neng's verse expresses the Southern School. The first is the way of gradual awakening, the second the way of sudden awakening. These are not simply different Chinese schools of Zen, but are representative of two basic spiritual tendencies in human beings. Another way of putting this is to say that the religious life comes, to some extent, from the recognition that suffering is endemic to all existence. This suffering arises out of a basic duality, and because of it, a yearning arises for a unity that will enable us to transcend duality and so be liberated from the suffering. Different religions have different ways and names, but all seek a consummating unity.

The Buddha's revolution cut through the very notion of duality, saying that it arises simply from ignorance. The "cutting through" is accomplished by prajna, or, more simply, prajna is awakening from the sleep of duality. Naturally, each person has to find for himself or herself this living resolution, and, because of our inherent inertia (arising from the illusion of duality itself), a tendency to revert to dualism reasserts itself again and again. Throughout the history of religion, including Buddhism and even Zen Buddhism, the basic teaching that dualism is illusory is rediscovered over and over.

The revolution of the Mahayana School, particularly the Prajnaparamita School (and Rinzai Zen, which is based upon it), was to turn away from any underlying unity, whether in the form of a self or of a God. The revolution is expressed in the fourth of the four great vows of the bodhisattva, "The Great Way of Buddha I vow to attain." Through this vow, to break through the substratum that samadhi was said to reveal, prajna came to have supreme importance.

Prajna as the Primary Virtue

Toward the end of the *Prajnaparamita* it says:

> *The Bodhisattva, holding to nothing whatever,*
> *but dwelling in prajna wisdom, is freed of delusive hindrance,*
> *rid of the fear bred by it, and reaches clearest nirvana.*

It is by *dwelling in prajna wisdom*, not by dwelling in some blessed state of rest, that we may find an end to suffering. Just as full Buddhahood has, with the advent of Mahayana, replaced samadhi as the ultimate goal of practice, prajna has become the primary virtue, replacing dhyana or samadhi. It is as a consequence of prajna, the sutra tells us, that the bodhisattva "saw the emptiness of all five skandhas," which are the physical body, emotion, intellect, will, and consciousness.

Prajna is *knowing* that is aroused, heightened, fulfilled, by being freed from all *knowledge*, from all that is known. Heightened knowing would be like drawing a sword from its scabbard.

Nevertheless, when we talk about knowing, we must not infer that there is a self that knows or something that is known. Prajna is knowing which is its own being. This is also the meaning of the word *bodhisattva*: *bodhi* meaning "knowing," and *sattva* meaning "being." In other words, neither does *someone* know, (*anatman*) nor is *something* known (*anicca*).

In saying that prajna is knowing which is its own being, or knowing-being, we must not even infer that knowing is an ever-abiding substratum that supports what is known. It is not a mirror that is there all the time. Dogen said that Buddha nature, what I am calling knowing-being, is impermanent. This is implicit in the expression *knowing-being*. It is because we believe we know *something* that knowing seems to be permanent. Furthermore, it is because knowing-being is not a substratum that we can say all things are empty.

Because this is such a vital point, let us use an analogy to help clarify it further. We see a film: a man and a woman fall in love, they pass through various difficult experiences, they separate and are finally reunited. All this occurs before our eyes. All the passion, romance, tension, terror and anger, relief and love, arise out of what is projected onto the screen. Yet what is really projected onto the screen is simply different intensities and modifications of light, which comes from a projector. As we know, light is not "something"; it is an *ongoingness* brought about by a passage of energy across a positive and a negative pole. The energy is analogous to knowing-being, the light is analogous to consciousness, the projected pictures are analogous to experience. The totality is what we call our life.

But where in all of this can something be found that endures? Someone might say that the energy endures. But is energy something? As a physicist would point out, in the world of light, time, space, energy, and mass do not exist. Light is constant velocity that knows no rest.

We are apt to say that what cannot be grasped by the senses and cannot be measured in some way does not exist, or has no reality. But in our analogy it is precisely what cannot be grasped, the world of light, that is the basis of our experience. Likewise, the Prajnaparamita School would say, "what has no form is the basis of form."

The essence of Buddhism, then, according to the Prajnaparamita, is prajna, knowing "purified" of all that is known. What does the word *purified* mean here? Let us use another analogy. A mirror and its reflections cannot be separated; we cannot put the mirror over here and the reflections over there. But the mirror and the reflections are not the same, and it is possible to *discern* the mirror that lies "beyond" the reflections, in this way the mirror is "purified" of its reflections.

Suppose you are looking at your face in the mirror. You do not see the mirror, you just see your face. Nevertheless, it is possible to look through the reflections and study the mirror. For instance, you might want to see if the mirror has a slight warp that could cause distortions. One can say that the mirror and the reflections are in different orders of reality. The mirror has one reality, the reflections have another. The mirror, furthermore, could be said to be higher than, or beyond, the reflections.

In a similar way, knowing and what is known cannot be separated, although it is possible "to discern" knowing beyond what is known. This discerning is what is called "waking up." All we know are reflections of knowing, and just as the mirror is not the reflections, knowing is not what is known. This means that nowhere in all that is known or experienced can knowing be found. Knowing occupies a different order from all that is known; it is higher than or beyond all that is known. We must be careful, as Hui Neng's verse made clear, not to take the analogy any further. Knowing is not a constant, underlying substratum; it is not a being that knows. Knowing has no before or after. Knowing is constantly emerging, constantly surging up.

So *Prajnaparamita* means "to get to the other shore by way of prajna," or "to get beyond knowing things to pure knowing (which means knowing without content).” In the first koan of a collection called the *Hekiganroku*, or *Blue Cliff Records*, a conversation is recorded between an emperor, whose name was Wu, and Bodhidharma, the first Chinese Zen patriarch. This conversation puts in a nutshell all that we have been saying in this chapter. The emperor asks, “What is your teaching?” And Bodhidharma replies, “Vast emptiness and not a thing that can be called holy.” The emperor then asks, “Who are you?” And Bodhidharma declares, “Not-knowing,” usually translated as “I don’t know.” Vast emptiness without a thing that can be called holy is not-knowing and not-knowing, in this instance, means not knowing something, or knowing without content or definition, vast emptiness. The problem with the word *vast* is that it seems to refer to an extended space. But what Bodhidharma means by *vast* is no barriers, no obstructions of any kind. The mind does not rest upon anything.

1. The prefix *pra-*, according to the dictionary, means “fulfilled.” According to Guenther and Chogyam Trungpa, the word *pra* and the Tibetan word *rab*, which is used to translate the Sanskrit *pra*, both also mean “to heighten” or “intensify.” “Therefore,” they say, *“shes rab* [Tibetan] or *prajna* [Sanskrit] refers to an intensification of the cognitive processes. The cognitive potentiality that is present in everyone is to be developed, intensified and brought to its highest pitch. To bring this potential to its highest pitch means to release it, to free it, from all the extraneous material that has accumulated.” See Herbert V. Guenther and Chogyam Trungpa, *The Dawn of Tantra* (Berkeley: Shambhala, 1975), pp. 27-28.
2. Master Hakuin, in his famous verse *In Praise of Zazen*, says, “Observing the precepts, repentance and giving, the countless good deeds, and the way of right living, all come from zazen. True zazen is prajna.”
3. *Theravada* means “Teaching of the Elders.” *-Yana* means “small vehicle,” and *hina* and *maha* mean “small” and “great” respectively, so *Hinayana* means “small vehicle” and *Mahayana* means “great vehicle.” With the Prajnaparamita School, a major shift occurred in Buddhism, from the search for ultimate samadhi to the search for full awakening as Buddha.

The Theravadins, to whom the Mahayanists refer as Hinayanists, claimed that, because the sutras on which their teachings are based came from the mouth of Buddha, as remembered by Ananda, theirs is the true teaching. The Mahayana sutras came long after the deaths of both Buddha and Ananda, therefore the Mahayanist teachings must be heretical. But for the reasons I give, the teaching is its own validation.

CHAPTER 3

PRAJNAPARAMITA HRIDAYA:
HEART OF PERFECT WISDOM

Magnificent! Magnificent!
No one knows the final word,
The ocean bed's aflame
Out of the void leap wooden lambs
A DEATH POEM

The Bodhisattva of Compassion, from the depths of
    prajna wisdom,
saw the emptiness of all five skandhas
and sundered the bonds of suffering.
Know then: Form here is only emptiness,
    emptiness only form.
Form is no other than emptiness,
emptiness no other than form.
Feeling, thought and choice, consciousness itself,
    are the same as this.
Dharmas here are empty; all are the primal void.
None are born or die,
Nor are they stained or pure, nor do they wax or wane.
So in emptiness no form, no feeling, thought, or choice,
nor is there consciousness.
No eye, ear, nose, tongue, body, mind;
no color, sound, smell, taste, touch, or what the mind takes
hold of, nor even act of sensing.
No ignorance or end of it, nor all that comes of ignorance:
no withering, no death, no end of them.

nor is there pain, or cause of pain, or cease in pain,
or noble path to lead from pain.
Not even wisdom to attain, attainment too is emptiness.
So know that the Bodhisattva, holding to nothing whatever,
but dwelling in prajna wisdom, is freed of delusive hindrance,
rid of the fear bred by it, and reaches clearest nirvana.
All Buddhas of past and present, Buddhas of future time,
through faith in prajna wisdom come to full enlightenment.
Know then the great dharani, the radiant, peerless mantra,
the supreme, unfailing mantra, the *Prajnaparamita*,
whose words allay all pain.
This is highest wisdom, true beyond all doubt,
know and proclaim its truth:
Gate, gate, paragate, parasamgate, bodhi, sva-ha!

The *Prajnaparamita Hridaya* is the condensation of a work that originally had a hundred thousand lines. This was abridged to eight thousand lines and finally to the Hridaya. *Hridaya* means "heart" or "essence." And the *Prajnaparamita Hridaya* is, therefore, often referred to as the *Heart Sutra*. Yet the *Prajnaparamita Hridaya* can also be condensed. Traditionally, it is said that it can be condensed to the letter *A*. From the point of view of people who are working on koans as the basis of their practice, it makes more sense to say that it can be reduced to *Mu!* Mu! is the essence of the *Prajnaparamita*. This means that a study of the *Prajnaparamita* can give us background for the practice with Mu.

The koan "Mu!" is the first in a collection of forty-eight koans called the *Mumonkan*.[1] According to this koan, a monk asked Zen Master Joshu, "Does a dog have the Buddha nature?" and Joshu replied, "Mu!" Tradition has it that all beings are Buddha. Why, then, does Joshu say "Mu!" which means "No"? The same question can be asked of the *Prajnaparamita*. It says, "No eye, ear, nose, tongue." Why does it say this when it is obvious that we do have eyes, ears, nose, and so on? In other words, both the sutra and the koan push us to investigate what we usually take for granted. What does it mean to say "I" "have" eyes, ears, and nose? What does it mean to say that a dog has, or does not have, the Buddha nature?

"The Bodhisattva of Compassion, from the depths of prajna wisdom, saw the emptiness of all five skandhas"

Because this is a sutra addressed to prajna, or wisdom, we must ask why it refers to Avalokita, the bodhisattva of *compassion,* and not to Manjusri, the bodhisattva of *wisdom,* or *prajna.* Why is Avalokita the chief protagonist of the *Prajnaparamita* and not Manjusri? Manjusri was a chief protagonist of another sutra, *The Perfection of Wisdom in Seven Hundred Lines.* Indeed, among the wisdom sutras, it is only in the *Heart Sutra* that the bodhisattva of compassion appears. Why is this? Wisdom without compassion is sterile, cold, and remote; compassion without wisdom is sentimental. Having the bodhisattva of compassion as the protagonist of a sutra concerned with wisdom brings home the point that both are essential.

One of the unjust criticisms of Zen is that it is selfish. Is it not selfish, people ask, to be concerned with one's own salvation when so much suffering exists in the world? Yes, it is. But what is this "one's own salvation"? Can I really practice Zen for my own salvation? Would not such a practice be based upon a fundamental contradiction? Compassion is essentially involvement. And involvement is only possible if one can see into the emptiness of all five skandhas.

The five skandhas are all that go to make up a human being. Prajna, let us remember, means to arouse the mind without resting it on anything. Arousing the mind in this way is itself "seeing into the emptiness of all five skandhas." Zen Master Hakuin, in his verses in *In Praise of Zazen,* says the same thing in a slightly different way: "True self is no-self, our own self is no-self." Arousing the mind means no self to be awakened, no self to be saved. To see the emptiness of the five skandhas would be to see into the illusory nature of the self, the root and cause of selfishness.

One can be compassionate or completely involved only after one has clearly seen that true self is no-self. Far from being self-ish, the activity that leads to seeing this is the most unselfish activity of all. To see that true self is no-self requires that one let go of the claims "me first," "I am important," "I am the one who matters." You may substitute the cause, the flag, the family, the company, some ideal or god for the word *I*, but *I* lies behind and gives significance to all of these. As Nisargadatta Maharaj, the Indian sage who died in the early 1980s, said, "Do not pretend that you love others as yourself. Unless you have realized them as one with yourself, you cannot love them. . . . Your love of others is the result of self-knowledge, not its cause. Without self-real-ization, no virtue is genuine." Self-realization is the realization that true self is no-self.

Compassion is possible when we are able to let the welfare of another be as important as our own. It has been said that love is to be one with another in joy, compassion to be one with another in sorrow. In order to be compassionate, in order to let the welfare of another take precedence over one's own welfare, the "one" that is oneself must be attenuated. While one is hard, forceful, predomi-nant, selfishness will always be present. As one practices, as one sees into the emptiness of all five skandhas, the heart begins to melt, the barriers separating one from others become transparent. In this way, compassion is nurtured.

I remember asking a Tibetan lama, "What is Buddhism?" He answered that it is the development of wisdom and compassion. "How, then," I asked, "does one develop compassion?" "Through wisdom," he replied. "How are we to develop wisdom?" He said, "By seeing that all things are empty."

By introducing the sutra from the point of view of the bod-hisattva of compassion, all of what we have said above is brought into focus.

The Five Skandhas: Nothing Abides,
All Is Impermanent

The word *skandha* means, literally, "group," "aggregate," or "heap"; perhaps the modern term "system" would be the most appropriate. These five skandhas make up what we call the person, or personality. In order, they are *rúpa, vedaná, samjná, samskara,* and *vijnana. Rúpa* means "form." The word "form," however, should be understood in its widest context. It corresponds not simply with the word *thing*, but instead with anything that can be perceived, imagined, or known. *Vedaná* could be translated as "sensation." *Samjná* sometimes is used to mean "perception," but because *samjná* literally means "knowing together," it might better be called "idea."[2] *Samskara* sometimes means "mental formations," such as concepts and ideas, but the word really has more to do with the dynamic aspect of the "person" and includes attention, volition, discrimination, concentration, and so on, so it is more appropriately called motivation. *Vijnana* means "divided awareness" (*vi* = divided; *jna* = awareness) or "consciousness." It is a word that is used a lot in the *Lankavatara Sutra*, so we shall be coming back to it in Chapter 6.

When the sutra says that the Bodhisattva saw that the five are empty, it means that what we have always looked upon as the individual, or person, has no innate substance, no soul, spirit, or self. The characteristics of the skandhas are birth, old age, death, duration, and change. In other words, nothing abides, all is impermanent. I am reminded of the saying of Henri Bergson, "It is not so that things change. It is rather that things are change." Saying that the characteristics of the skandhas are birth, old age, and so on is similar to saying that the five skandhas are without essence, that is, without being (*anicca*) and so impermanent, are without self (*anatman*) and so without a permanent "I," and are the cause of suffering (*dukkha*).

"The Bodhisattva of Compassion, from the depths of prajna wisdom, saw the emptiness of all five skandhas and sundered the bonds of suffering."

Again, we return to the first noble truth of Buddhism: The basis of life is suffering. Suffering is intrinsic to the five skandhas because, although they are empty of self-nature, although they are impermanent, we behave as if a self-nature were inherent in them, and, furthermore, as if this self-nature were immortal. In other words, according to the second noble truth, our suffering arises because of *desire*, the desire to find a self-nature, to be someone, somewhere, for some reason. Furthermore, we want all of this not only for the time being, but for always. We want to be absolute, by which we mean to be eternally someone, somewhere, for some reason.

Buddha began his pilgrimage to the truth when he met the impermanence of the five skandhas in the form of a sick man, an old man, and a dead man, the three testaments to our impermanence. At the time he met these three, Buddha was still clinging to the belief in a self and so was dismayed by what he saw. It is this suffering, this dismay, the sense of our utter vulnerability, of the precariousness of our existence, and of its apparent contingency that drives us into practice.

These first lines of the sutra sum up the whole of practice, that is to say, we must see into the emptiness of all five skandhas and so sunder the bonds of suffering. Koan practice, particularly with the first koans, such as "Mu!" and "Who am I?" is a direct route to seeing the emptiness of all five skandhas, to seeing into no-self. The Japanese word for "no-self" is *muga*, but *mu* is enough. *Mu!* is no-self. Asking earnestly, honestly, and tirelessly, "Who am I?" melts down the illusion of the skandha shells and allows the light of truth to shine out.

**"Form here is only emptiness, emptiness only form.
Form is no other than emptiness, emptiness no
other than form."**

This is the very heart of the teaching: form is emptiness; emptiness
is form. *Emptiness*, a key term in the *Prajnaparamita*, is the coun-
terpart to prajna, though it is important to not make the mistake of
saying that prajna is "seeing into emptiness." "Seeing" is *already*
prajna, and prajna is already emptiness. This is true also of hearing, tasting, feeling, smelling—all are modes of knowing, of prajna,
and therefore all are empty. To say that prajna is seeing into emptiness is to make something of both "seeing" and emptiness. It is, to
use an expression of the philosopher Alfred North Whitehead, to
commit the fallacy of misplaced concreteness. The word *emptiness*
is provisional, and one can only use it truly if one can see that
emptiness, too, is empty. In other words, emptiness has no ontological status and is not an *absence*. One commentator has sug-
gested that emptiness is the mode of being of form.[3] It might be
truer to say that form has no mode of being of its own, which is
why it is called empty.

When it is said that "form *is* emptiness," we must not look
upon the *is* as the *is* of identity. Form is not identical with emptiness. Form is form, emptiness is emptiness. Even so, form is
empty. We can use again our analogy of a mirror: the mirror is its
reflections; the reflections are the mirror. But the reflections are
reflections; the mirror is the mirror. To say that the mirror is the
reflections is to say that one cannot see the reflections without the
mirror: one cannot see form without emptiness because, as I said
in the previous paragraph, the seeing is emptiness. Just as it is in
the nature of a mirror to reflect, the nature of knowing or seeing is
to know, to see.

The statement "Form is emptiness, emptiness is form" must

not be looked upon as symmetrical. If, for example, I say, "A is B, B is A," this statement is symmetrical—I am saying the same thing in two different ways. By contrast, if I say, "The reflection is the mirror," I am saying something quite different than if I say, "The mirror is the reflection." The reflection is dependent upon the mirror for its very existence; the mirror is dependent upon the reflection only in order to be able to function as a mirror. The reflection is totally dependent upon something else: the mirror. The mirror is totally dependent upon its own self-nature, its potential to reflect.

In a similar way, if I say, "Form is emptiness," I mean that the form, to be that form, is dependent upon emptiness. If I see a tree, the form of the tree is dependent upon my seeing. The form of the tree is different depending on where I am. It is different when viewed from a helicopter a hundred feet in the air from when it is viewed from the ground ten feet away, or from within its branches. Seeing, as I have pointed out, is already emptiness; seeing is already prajna. This will become clearer when we consider other sutras. Although "seeing the tree" is one seamless whole, this is not enough because two different aspects are involved: "seeing" and "the tree." Simply to say that form is emptiness would reduce the *Prajnaparamita* to an idealist philosophy. So it is said, "Emptiness is form." Another way of saying this is saying that knowing is dynamic; it has to know. If we are going to see, we always have to see something! Trees, birds, roads, cars, factories—everything and anything is reflected without fail.

However, explanations fail to help us see into the real meaning of the statement, "Emptiness is form; form is emptiness." To see into the truth that "form is emptiness" requires a leap, or, to use an expression from the *Diamond Sutra*, it requires us to "arouse the mind without resting it upon anything." Because this leap lies at the very heart of the *Prajnaparamita Sutras* and Rinzai Zen, as well as of koan practice, let us make a short detour to look more deeply into its meaning.

Spiritual Irony

To say, "form is emptiness, emptiness is form" is to express a kind of *spiritual irony*, and an understanding of how irony is effective in enabling us to make this leap will help us to appreciate what is involved in this statement. Both the sutras and the koans are used to encourage students to make this leap, and some parts of the sutras that we shall be studying, as well as Zen koans, can be called spiritual irony.

To understand spiritual irony, let us first look at ordinary irony. During the 1960s, a bumper sticker read, "An atomic war could ruin your whole day." We must not overlook the word *could* in this warning. Most people would say that an atomic war would be the end of civilization as we know it, or even the end of the world. Why does this sticker simply warn us that it "*could* ruin your whole day"? A bride's day could be ruined if some paint were spilled on her wedding dress. An executive's day could be ruined if at the last minute some basic errors were found in a report that she or he was about to present to the board of directors. A golfer's day could be ruined by an attack of bursitis. But an atomic war! Could anyone believe that an atomic war could "ruin our day?" The enormity of an atomic war and the banality of a ruined day are incommensurate. Of course, an atomic war *would* ruin one's day! But how can one say such a thing? As we ponder this saying, we find ourselves caught in a loop: it is foolish to say it, but it is true nevertheless; it is foolish to say it. . . . The only way out of the loop is to leap to a higher viewpoint. This is similar to the leap that one makes in looking at an ambiguous picture.

This is a picture of a young lady and an old lady. To see the old lady and then the young lady, one "leaps" from a view of the old lady

ZEN & THE SUTRAS

to that of the young lady and vice versa. This leap from picture to picture is a leap sideways; it is a leap from one viewpoint to another, but at the same level. With irony, one leaps to a higher viewpoint.

What does this leap to a higher level imply? One gets out of the loop created by the bumper sticker by saying, "Ah! It is being ironical. What it is really saying is that the end of civilization is coming at the speed of an express train, yet this means about as much to you as stained dresses, erroneous reports, and stiff arms—things that can ruin your whole day!" In other words, with irony two incompatible ideas are brought together into a meaningful whole. We are uncomfortable with irony until we make the leap to a higher viewpoint.

Such explanations of irony are clumsy, pedestrian. This also is true if one tries to explain a joke. The reason irony is so effective is it says a great deal with very few words.

How does this apply to koans? A famous koan tells of the monk Joshu, who after a long, dangerous, exhausting journey, met a Zen master, Nansen, and asked him, "What is the Way?" Nansen replied, "Everyday mind is the way." Everyday mind was the very mind that Joshu had traveled so far, and had endured so much danger, to escape. When he asked Nansen, "What is the Way?" he was asking, "How can I escape from the suffering involved in everyday mind?" Yet Nansen replied, "Everyday mind is the way."

Like the bumper sticker, this koan contains two incompatibles: the way to spiritual emancipation and everyday mind. The contradiction in the two ideas of the bumper sticker can be resolved by leaping to a viewpoint from which one can look down upon those who are so immersed in the pettiness of their daily concerns that they do not see the train bearing destruction approaching at breakneck speed. The contradiction in the koan is also resolved by a leap. But this leap is made not to another, more embracing viewpoint but to *no viewpoint at all.*

In another koan, a monk goes to a master and asks, "Do not

give me words, do not give me silence, what is the truth?" Some spiritual teachers, Sri Aurobindo, for example, realizing the limitations of words, would remain silent. But this monk with his question takes away the possibility of silence. Yet if one cannot use words—and this would cover all forms of communication, including dancing and gesture—and one cannot use silence, then how is one to respond?

The *Prajnaparamita Hridaya* says, "Form is only emptiness." In this saying, two incompatible ideas, "form" and "emptiness," are brought together. We can resolve the contradiction by a leap, by "arousing the mind," but the leap is to no viewpoint, because the sutra goes on to say, "without resting upon anything." But how could we make a leap to no viewpoint at all? Would not *no viewpoint* be either a pure abstraction or a leap into nonsense?

Let us return to the bumper sticker for our answer. It does not say, "Wake up, you fools, leave your petty bickering and infantile concerns or else we shall all be destroyed." It just says, "An atomic war could ruin your whole day." Irony demands that we leap *while refusing to take the leap.* My explanation has, to some extent, weakened this ironical statement because it has provided a ladder by which to escape. Even so, it is in demanding a leap to a unifying viewpoint but refusing to allow this leap to be made, compelling the reader to remain with an implacable contradiction, that the strength of irony lies.

The *Prajnaparamita* says, "Form is only emptiness, emptiness only form." We must not be, as some scholars are, taken in by this anymore than we should be taken in by the bumper sticker. The sutra is not saying form is *identical* to emptiness, so whenever you come up against the word *emptiness* you can substitute the word *form*, or vice versa.

In case you think this trivial, let us translate the statement "Emptiness is form" using *mind* for "emptiness" and *matter* for "form." It would now read, "Mind is only matter," something that not a few modern scientists would agree with. It would also say, "Matter is only mind." Not a few, including some other respected scientists, would agree with this also.[4] My guess is that these latter scientists are not taken in by the irony of existence but are comfortable working within it. By contrast, many scientists who claim that mind is only matter, those, for example, doing research into artificial life, artificial intelligence, and the workings of the brain, *are* taken in by it. Consider the following statement by Nobel Prize winner Francis Crick: "Your joys and your sorrows, your memories and your ambitions, your sense of personal identity and free will, are in fact no more than the behavior of a vast assembly of nerve cells and their associated molecules."[5] He misses the irony and says mind *is* matter, emptiness is form.

We shall see many examples of spiritual irony in what follows. Each example will demand that a leap—a leap to no viewpoint— be made, but that leap, because it is not made, will give the saying immense power.

"Feeling, thought and choice, consciousness itself, are the same as this."

Feeling, thought, choice, and consciousness are the other four skandhas. Form is basic to them all. Feelings, thoughts, decisions, even consciousness are forms, although of increasingly subtle kinds. If form is empty, then feeling, thought, choice, and consciousness are empty, too. The five skandhas are analyzed at length in a famous Buddhist psychological text called the *Abhidharmakosa*, in which it is said that because the self is a structure of five systems, it can have no abiding nature. But the *Prajnaparamita* is going further still by saying that even these five systems are themselves without self-nature, that is to say, they, too, are empty. The *Prajnaparamita* appears to undermine the whole teaching of the *Abhidharmakosa*, but only to those who miss the spiritual irony.

"Dharmas here are empty, all are the primal void."

Dharma is one of those words for which it is almost impossible to find an adequate English equivalent. In this instance, the word could be translated as "phenomenon." In other words, all things, all phenomena, are empty, all are the primal void. Mountains, trees, cars, people, dogs, cats, airplanes—all are the primal void. However, *primal void* must not be taken to be mere absence. While it is true that form is empty, emptiness is also form.

None are born or die,
nor are they stained or pure,
nor do they wax or wane.

These lines seem to undermine another basic teaching of Buddhism, unless one bears in mind all that we said about spiritual irony. It is one of the basic axioms of Buddhism that everything that has form was born and is destined to grow old, decline, and die. Furthermore, it seems evident that everything is either pure or defiled. Yet the *Prajnaparamita* says that the dharmas are not born, they do not grow or decline, neither do they die, and this is so because they are empty.

It seems so obvious that things do come into and go out of existence; we are alive or dead. A koan in the *Hekiganroku* tells of a master and a disciple who go to pay their respects to another disciple who has just died. When they arrive at the house in which the dead man is lying, the disciple taps the coffin and asks the master, "Alive or dead?" The master replies, "I won't say! I won't say!" Why does the master reply "I won't say! I won't say!" when it seems the answer is so obvious? Surely it must be one or the other, alive or dead. Is an alternative to alive or dead possible; is an alternative to being or not being possible, or something or nothing?

Dogen said, "Once firewood is reduced to ashes, it cannot return to firewood; but we should not think of ashes as the poten-

tial state of firewood or vice versa. Ash is completely ash and firewood is firewood. Similarly, when people die, they cannot return
to life; but in Buddhist teaching we never say that life changes into
death."[6] In other words, we cannot blur the lines between life and
death, even with such myths as reincarnation and heaven. These,
too, are forms; these, too, are empty.

If we take away life and death, something and nothing, being
and not being, what is left? It is toward this that the sutra is pointing us. "Beyond" something and nothing is emptiness; "beyond"
being and not being is knowing. Does a dog have a Buddha nature?
It seems that the answer must be yes or no. Joshu says, "No!" but
this "No!" is a fulfillment, not a negation. What, then, is beyond life
and death? If dharmas are not even born, nor do they die, what
remains? We cannot answer this question with words and thoughts.
This is why the master says, "I won't say!" However, we must not
overlook the fact that he says, "I won't say!" not "I cannot say!"

"So in emptiness no form, no feeling, thought, or choice, nor is there consciousness."

Once again it is emphasized, no form, feeling, thought, or choice,
indeed, no consciousness even. In such a compact sutra, a repetition like this means what is being said must be very important
indeed. In other words, we must meditate on this sentence. These
words are not the expression of a Buddhist dogma. This is not a
catechism, a credo. It is a challenge, a call to awaken.

"No eye, ear, nose, tongue, body, mind"

We chant the *Prajnaparamita Hridaya* repeatedly during retreats,
or *sesshins,* as they are called in Japan. But how many people taking part in the sesshin, chanting the sutra, ever ask themselves
what these words mean? One day, a young monk, after the two had
chanted the *Prajnaparamita* together, asked his teacher, "I have a

nose, ears, eyes; why does the *Prajnaparamita* say, 'No ears, eyes, nose'?" His teacher replied, "Your question is too deep for me. I shall have to introduce you to a Zen master." If I should ask someone, "Is the room we are in at the moment real?" the answer almost always would be, "Yes!" This seems self-evident. But if I then ask, "How do you know the room is real?" the person will say, "Because I see it and can touch it." But the *Prajnaparamita* says no eye exists with which to see, no hand with which to touch. Similarly, most people believe that they are the body. But the sutra says, "No body." Again we are challenged. If one truly understands the question, one can never sleep in peace again. It is as though the sutra sprinkles crumbs in the bed.

One could well retreat and say, "I am the mind." The French philosopher Descartes used this way out. He said that I can doubt everything—even, if you like, that I am the body—but I cannot doubt that I am because I think, and to doubt is to think. But what is it that thinks? The mind? When one uses this word *mind*, what is one referring to? I am not talking about the dictionary definition but what is the subjective experience of mind. Such a question offers an interesting challenge. How do we study the mind. Not the contents of the mind, but the mind itself?

Consider this dialogue—it has been made into a koan that appears in the *Mumonkan*—in which the Second Patriarch, Hui K'o, asks Bodhidharma, "Your servant's mind knows no peace. I beg you, please give it peace." Bodhidharma says, "Bring me your mind and I will set it at peace." Hui K'o replies, "I have searched for my mind everywhere but cannot find it anywhere." With what did he search for the mind?

"No ignorance or end of it, nor all that comes of ignorance"

Ignorance is one of the three *klesás,* or "sins" of Buddhism, to use a rough translation of this word. The other two are anger and greed. Ignorance, though, is the principal klesá. Ignorance is the root from which the tree of self, personality, and selfishness grows. Cut this root and one is free. But how does one cut the root?

The meaning of ignorance is expressed succinctly by a basic koan: "Who am I?" All our troubles start because we cannot truly answer this question. We cannot answer it because of ignorance. This is so not because we cannot answer the question, but, more importantly, because we do not even know how to ask it. We do not know how to ask it because, invariably, a hidden assumption, which we take completely for granted and rarely examine, is included in the question: Given that I am, then what, or who, am I? "Given that I am" is ignorance, because this implies that I am *something*. "Ignorance" and the assumption that "I am something" are not two. Because I constantly assume that I am something, I ignore, turn my back upon, my true self.

The *Prajnaparamita* goes much further than simply saying that the root cause is ignorance; it also says that ignorance is *empty*. How do you get rid of ignorance? Not by study and application, nor by meditation or concentration or contemplation. These may lay the groundwork, bring you to the door, even perhaps open the door, but you still must enter. Another question, similar to asking how one gets rid of ignorance, is: How do you get rid of the fairy who is not in the corner? By seeing that no fairy stands in the corner. Paradoxically, it is only by seeing the illusory nature of ignorance that one can get beyond ignorance. So "No ignorance, no end of it, nor all that comes of ignorance."

"no withering, no death"

When Buddha saw the sick man, the old man, and the dead man they set him on the Way. But the *Prajnaparamita* says that no withering occurs, nor can one die. Step by step, it seems, the *Prajnaparamita* refutes the whole of Buddha's teaching. In a similar way, it seems that Joshu, when he replies to the monk's question about whether the dog has a Buddha nature, is refuting the most basic teaching of Buddha, who at the time of his great Awakening exclaimed, "Wonder of wonders, all beings are endowed with the Buddha nature." Hakuin Zenji, in his verse *In Praise of Zazen*, echoes this exclamation when he says, "From the beginning all beings are Buddha." Yet Joshu, in response to the monk's question, says no Buddha nature. Joshu's "Mu!" which means "No!" is the same as saying *"no* eye, ear, nose, tongue, and so on." It is the same no as in *"no* withering, *no* death, *no* end of them." Even so, we cannot simply take Joshu's "Mu!" literally.

When this dialogue occurred, Joshu was probably an old man who had worked on himself for a long lifetime. It is unlikely that he would have contradicted one of the most profound insights of Buddha. So what can Joshu have meant? On another occasion, in reply to the same question, "Does a dog have Buddha nature?" he said, "Yes!" Remember spiritual irony? Joshu's "Mu!" and the *Prajnaparamita's* "no eye, ear, nose, tongue" and "no withering, no death" are also spiritual irony.

"Nor is there pain, or cause of pain, or cease in pain, or noble path to lead from pain."

What? Is the *Prajnaparamita* refuting the four noble truths of Buddhism?

The four noble truths read as follows:

Suffering

Birth is suffering, old age is suffering, sickness is suffering, death is suffering, likewise sorrow, grief and lamentation and despair. To be together with things we do not like is suffering, to be separated from things we like, that also is suffering. Not to get what we want, that also is suffering. In a word, this body, this fivefold mass [the five skandhas] based upon grasping, that is suffering.

The Cause of Suffering
It is that craving which gives rise to fresh rebirth and, bound by greed for pleasure, now here, now there, finds ever-fresh delight. It is the sensual craving, the craving for individual existence, the craving to have done with individual existence.

The End of Suffering
It is the utter, passionless cessation of, the giving up, the forsaking, the release from, the absence of longing for this craving.

The Noble Path
Right views, right aim, right speech, right action, right living, right effort, right mindfulness, right contemplation.

The *Prajnaparamita* says, "no pain," no suffering. However, it continues by saying, "no cease in pain" nor any way out of pain. The *Prajnaparamita* is pointing to Nirvana, but not the Nirvana that has so often been criticized for being negative and nihilistic. People have looked upon Nirvana as extinction, complete absence. I remember Yasutani roshi saying to me that, with awakening, "nothing is changed." He extended his hands with the right hand on top of the left. Then he said, "But everything is changed." And in a swift movement he turned his hands over so that left was now on the right. Nirvana is extinction, but it is the extinction of ignorance. With Nirvana, life, and all that makes up life, is still the same, but it is changed radically, in a way that cannot be imagined or conceived.

"Not even wisdom to attain, attainment too is emptiness."

If one can speak of a goal in practice, it would be to see into one's true nature. Would that not be to attain wisdom? No. Seeing into one's true nature is the end of attainment. It is the end of seeking. In one of the koans of the *Mumonkan,* a monk, Ganto, says of his teacher, Tokusan, "He has not gained the last word of Zen."

Ganto says this to Seppo, a brother monk, who no doubt thinks that Ganto is putting Tokusan down. On the contrary, Ganto is saying that Tokusan has seen into the same truth taught by the *Prajnaparamita* when it says, "Not even wisdom to attain, attainment too is emptiness." The last word of Zen is that there is no last word of Zen.

> **"So know that the Bodhisattva, holding to nothing whatever, but dwelling in prajna wisdom, is freed of delusive hindrance, rid of the fear bred by it, and reaches clearest nirvana."**

In this passage we see the full irony of the *Prajnaparamita*. After having systematically negated all feelings, all thought, all choice, and after declaring, "Not even wisdom to attain," it says that the bodhisattva is freed from fear by dwelling in prajna wisdom. The key to this section is "holding to nothing whatever," no self, no thing. It is in this way that one must work with the *Prajnaparamita* and also with the koans. All koans start from holding to nothing whatever. The first koans, "Mu!" or "Who am I?" or "The sound of one hand clapping," open us to what "holding to nothing whatever" means. The rest of the koans deepen this realization and so allow a constant enrichment to occur.

> **"All Buddhas of past and present, Buddhas of future time, through faith in prajna wisdom come to full enlightenment."**

Prajna is the mother of all Buddhas, including the seven legendary Buddhas. It is prajna that gives birth to Buddha. "Faith in prajna wisdom" is somewhat redundant, because faith already is prajna wisdom. Each of us is Buddha; each of us has prajna as mother. Each of us is already and always fully present. Nothing lies outside of us. Each of us knows this. Our true nature is knowing. It is like a light that shines by itself, and this light that shines by itself is faith. Each of us knows that nothing lies outside of us, and this is prajna. The problem is that when it is put like this we have the impression that something is known. Let us, then, instead, use a *mondo*, question and answer. Someone asked Zen Master Joshu, "What is my essence?" Joshu replied, "The tree sways, the bird flies about, the fish leaps, the water is muddy."

"Know then the great dharani, the radiant, peerless mantra, the supreme, unfailing mantra, the *Prajnaparamita*, whose words allay all pain. This is highest wisdom, true beyond all doubt, know and proclaim its truth: Gate, gate, paragate, parasamgate, bodhi, sva-ha!"

The *Prajnaparamita* ends with this radiant, peerless mantra. The word *mantra* means "protection for the mind." A mantra is a phrase, or even just a single word, that one repeats during meditation or daily activities. The simplest mantra is just counting the breaths. Here is one way to understand the value of a mantra: Suppose that a group of people wants to do something but they have no leader. The group could well end up arguing among themselves, and nothing would get done. Suppose someone with authority were to appoint a leader of the group. The group would coalesce around the leader and could then do what needs to be done. Our mind, too, is full of conflicting thoughts that often nullify each other and cause us great tension and pain. By having one supreme thought, the rest are able to coalesce around it, and so harmony is restored.

Another way of thinking about the value of a mantra is that the random, negative thoughts that plague us require a certain kind of energy. If that energy is being used to recite the mantra, it will not be available for these thoughts.

The mantra of the *Prajnaparamita* has a certain rhythm, the rhythm of the heartbeat: "Gate, gate, paragate, parasamgate, bodhi, sva-ha!" It can be repeated continuously, like the continuous beating of the heart. If it is used as an adjunct to meditation, this mantra is most often in time with the breathing. In other words, the mantra can merge with the two basic rhythms of life: the beat of the heart and the rise and fall of the breath. In order to be able truly to use and benefit from the mantra, it is best to work with a qualified teacher.

This, however, is the most mechanical and uninspired way to use a mantra, of value to those who are very distracted and need a focus for their practice. But we must not overlook the fact that the mantra comes at the end of a profound and subtle sutra. It should, therefore, preferably be used within the context of the sutra. *Gate, gate* means "gone, gone." *Paragate* means "gone beyond." *Parasamgate* means "gone right beyond"—beyond all form, feeling, thought, and choice; beyond birth and death, wisdom and ignorance. Going beyond in this way brings us to bodhi. *Bodhi*, as we know, means "knowing," the light that shines by itself. Going right beyond awakens us to the light of the world.

Sva-ha! How wonderful!

1. I have commented upon the koans of the *Mumonkan* in *The World: A Gateway* (Boston: Charles Tuttle, 1996).

2. I make this distinction because elsewhere I have written at length about "idea," and this passage could provide a bridge to these writings.

3. Donald S. Lopez, Jr., *The Heart Sutra Explained* (Albany: State University of New York Press, 1988), p. 58.

4. For example, Professor John Archibald Wheeler, of the Institute of Theoretical Physics at the University of Texas at Austin, would say, "No elementary phenomenon is a real phenomenon until it is an observed phenomenon." Nick Herbert. *Quantum Reality: Beyond the New Physics* (New York: Anchor Books, 1987), p. 164.

5. Francis Crick and Christof Koch, "The Problem of Consciousness," *Scientific American* Special Issue, September 1992.

6. Dogen Zenji, *Shogogenzo, Genjokoan*, translated by Kosen Nishiyama and John Stevens (Sendai, Japan: Daihokkaikaku, 1975), p. 2.

CHAPTER 4

THE *DIAMOND SUTRA*

*Coming, going the duck
leaves no trace,
It needs no guide*

The *Diamond Sutra* is called, in Sanskrit, the *Vajrachche-dikaprajnaparamita Sutra,* and the last part of this name clearly places it in the Prajnaparamita tradition. The full translation of this name would be "Diamond Cutter of Supreme Wisdom." The word *vajra* can be translated as "thunderbolt" or as "diamond." In this instance it is translated as "diamond" or "diamond cutter." The diamond is the symbol of reality, because the diamond, like reality, is indestructible. It is a cutter because with it one is able to cut through all delusions, particularly the delusion of there being separated, isolated things. Thus the particular aspect of reality symbolized by the diamond is *sunyata,* or emptiness.

> One day, at breakfast time, the world-honored one put on his robe and, carrying his bowl, made his way into the great city of Shravasti to beg for his food. In the midst of the city he begged from door to door, according to the rule. This done, he returned to his retreat and ate his meal. When he had finished, he put away his robe and begging bowl, washed his feet, arranged his seat, and sat down.

This is how the *Diamond Sutra* begins. How different this is from the way so many other Mahayana sutras open. For example, the *Avatamsaka Sutra* begins in this way:

> As soon as the Buddha had entered this concentration, the magnificent pavilion became boundlessly vast, the surface of the earth appeared to be made of indestructible diamond, the surface of the ground covered with a net of all the finest jewels strewn around with flowers of many jewels with enormous gems strewn all over; it was adorned with sapphire pillars, with well-proportioned decorations of world-illuminating pearls of the finest water, with all kinds of gems combined in pairs, adorned with heaps of gold and jewels, with a dazzling array of turrets, arches, chambers, windows, and balconies.

What is so significant about the opening of the *Diamond Sutra* is that it presents Buddha as just another man. One is reminded of Nansen's reply to Joshu: Joshu asked him, "What is the Way?" and he replied, "Everyday mind is the Way." "Everyday mind is the Way" was surely one of the great contributions of Zen to the spiritual journey of humankind; nowhere else does one find this truth expressed so succinctly. No elaborate ritual, no deep theology, no mysticism or magic; just, "Everyday mind is the Way." One does not need a special mind to practice Zen, nor is it necessary to have special powers or specific emotions. As Joshu said later, "When I am hungry I eat; when I am tired I sleep." In the same way, without fanfare, Buddha is shown as just another monk, doing what monks of his time would have done.

However, we should not be taken in by the irony of this. Later in the dialogue with Joshu I just mentioned, Nansen says, "The Way is like vast space. Where is there room for good and bad, you and me, awakened and unawakened?" If we think of Buddha as an exalted person, someone who does not have the clay feet of human beings, if we believe that he has come down from the Tulsita Heavens, then of what use is he as a guide? If he and I do not share a common heritage of failings and possibilities, if he is on one track and I am on another, then I must look elsewhere for someone to help and inspire me in the midst of my ordinary human fallibility. It is precisely because Buddha is like you and me that he has value for us. However, Buddha is not *simply* an ordinary person. If I believed that he were, why should I take the time to penetrate the apparent contradictions that pervade this and other records of his teachings; why should I make the effort to understand what he says, or to practice in the way this understanding shows is necessary?

Buddha is an ordinary man, but he is not just an ordinary man. Perhaps the following exchange will shed some light on this paradox. Someone asked Yasutani roshi, "What is the difference between you and me?" Yasutani replied, "There is no difference except I know this." Buddha would have given the same reply. When Yasutani said, "There is no difference," he was saying the equivalent of "Everyday mind is the Way"; but when he said, "I know this," he was saying something similar to Nansen saying, "The Way is like vast space."

"The Irony of the Diamond Sutra"

The *Diamond Sutra* is full of irony. Its first, and one of its most striking ironies, is this. The sutra consists of a number of questions posed by Subhuti and Buddha's answers. The first question is, "World-honored one, if good men and good women seek the consummation of incomparable awakening, by what standards of judgment should they abide and how should they control their thoughts?" Buddha replies, "Bodhisattvas should discipline their thoughts thus, 'All living beings are caused by me to attain unbounded liberation Nirvana. Yet when vast, innumerable, immeasurable numbers of beings have been liberated, not one being has been liberated. Why is this? It is because no Bodhisattva who is a real Bodhisattva cherishes the idea of an ego-entity, a personality, a being, or a separated individuality.'"

This reply is full of irony because it contains two contradictions; one is hidden, one obvious. The hidden contradiction lies in Buddha saying, "All living beings are caused by *me* to attain unbounded liberation Nirvana." The obvious contradiction is "Yet when vast innumerable, immeasurable numbers of beings have been liberated, *not one being* has been liberated." Let us talk about these contradictions a little more.

It is a basic teaching of Buddhism that one person cannot purify another. In the *Dammapadda* it is said, "By oneself evil is done; by oneself one suffers. By oneself evil is undone; no one can purify another." When Buddha says, "All living beings are caused by *me* to attain unbounded liberation Nirvana," who is the *me*? We have just said that Buddha is an ordinary man and has no special powers. Furthermore, according to his own teaching, he does not have the power to liberate another. Why then does he make this statement? The answer to this question can be found in the other contradiction, which is the key to the sutra.

If there were two people—the first, Buddha, an ordinary monk who begs for his meals, who eats his food and then cleans his dishes; the second, someone who is seeking awakening and comes to the monk for instruction—the monk could in no way bring the seeker to awakening. He might encourage, inspire, guide, counsel, and support, but that would be as far as he could go. But if, as Nansen says, "The Way is like vast space. Where is there room for good and bad, you and me, awakened and unawakened?" then who is there to help, who is there to be helped? Buddha when he talks is not different from those to whom he talks; not only is he not different, he is not even separate from them. This is why he says, "No Bodhisattva who is a real Bodhisattva cherishes the idea of an ego-entity, a personality, a being, or a separated individuality." In other words, there are not two: the monk as one person and the seeker as another. There is not even one. But there is most certainly not nothing. What there is, is what Buddha calls "me."

Christ said, "No one comes to the Father except through 'me,'" and he also said, "'I' am the way, and the truth, and the life." Just as when Buddha used the word *me* it is unlikely that he was referring to Gautama Siddhartha, so it is unlikely that Christ meant Jesus of Nazareth when he used the words *me* and *I*. As the sutra says, there are no separate beings, no individual "me" or "I." It is in seeing this that we are liberated, or, to use the words of Christ, that we come to the Father. Seeing this *is* the truth and the way. When Buddha says that "all living beings are caused by me to attain unbounded liberation Nirvana," he is referring to "the way, and the truth, and the life" of which each of us is the manifestation.

Giving: Beyond Morality

The sutra goes on to say,

> If a Bodhisattva gives to, and helps, others because of a code of ethics or because of a set of principles, or because of morality, he is like a blind person groping in the shadows; but a Bodhisattva who gives to, and helps, others with a mind free of any ethical or moral notions is like a person with open eyes in the radiant glory of morning to whom all kinds of things are clearly visible.

The sutra then comments upon giving, or *dana*. Dana is the first of the six paramitas, of which prajna is the last. Very often the word *dana* is translated as "charity," but, thanks mainly to Charles Dickens, *charity* has come to mean just the opposite of what the *Diamond Sutra* is advocating. Charity so often implies duality: "*I* give *this* to *you*" The giver and the receiver are clearly different, and, implicitly, the giver is higher, while the receiver is lower. Later in the sutra Buddha says that the bodhisattva should save all living beings while realizing there are no living beings to save. Both this and the injunction to give without being attached to form have the same implication. As long as "I" give this to "you," or "I" help "you," a dualism is created, a dualism held in place by ethical and moral injunctions that insist it is one's duty to give; one is obliged to help.

Christ said that we must love our neighbors as ourselves, and this sutra teaches more or less the same thing. It says, "Furthermore, when giving, a Bodhisattva should be detached. That is to say one should give without being attached to form." If you need to be helped and I am obliged to help you, then we are separate, distinct, "you" and "me," a helper and a helped, and resentment of one kind or another is bound to arise. A bit of dialogue from a British television comedy series illustrates this beautifully: "I can't understand why everyone hates me. I haven't helped anyone in ages!" Milarepa, the great Tibetan sage, forbade his disciples to help others, saying that as long as there was an ego involved it could only end in disaster. Yet if someone slips, I cannot help but put out a hand; and if someone cries for help, who can refuse? It is at this spontaneous level that true help originates. Helping others in order to gain merit, and so be able to enter some heaven or other, is but giving that is attached to form. The sutra is not advocating that we not help others, but that we let go of the notion that "I" have to help "you."

How Does One Recognize Buddha?

Subhuti, the bodhisattva, then asks, "Is the Tathâgata to be recognized by some material characteristic?" Let us pause to consider this word *Tathâgata*. It is frequently used as a synonym for the word *Buddha*, in which case it refers to the person Shakyamuni, who is talking to Subhuti. However, as long as we hold to this understanding alone we shall never understand the *Diamond Sutra*, nor any other sutra. For one thing, as we know, Buddha has said, "No Bodhisattva who is a real Bodhisattva cherishes the idea of an ego-entity, a personality, a being, or a separated individuality." No Buddha who is a real Buddha cherishes the idea of being Buddha either.

Tathâgata is often translated as "thus come" or "thus gone." It is closely related to another word, *tathata*, which is usually translated as "suchness." The best translation of the word *Tathâgata*, however, is "comes to." One faints, and one comes to; one is in a daze or a dreamy state, and one comes to. In other languages it is necessary to say what it is one comes to. In French, for example, one must say, *on retourne à la conscience*, "one returns to consciousness." In English it is not necessary to say what one comes to. *Tathata*, as we have said, is translated as "suchness." Asking "Is the Tathâgata to be recognized by some material characteristic?" is like asking, "When one comes to in an ultimate way, to what does one come to?" This question is the same as "What is Mu?" or "Who am I?" or "What is my face before my parents were born?" Subhuti is asking how we can recognize the Tathâgata, whether in others or in ourselves.

Many people feel that they must have some special experience, or some particular understanding, which will indicate that they have come to awakening. Or they try to see some mark of awakening in someone who is awakened or try to find significance in the actions and words of this person, while in fact these actions or words have no such significance. Others act and talk ponderously, in the belief that doing so will indicate wisdom, or they dress differently, or wear long beards, or shave their heads, or act in a way that they feel denotes an awakened person. But as Buddha says, "The Tathâgata cannot be recognized by any material characteristic. Wherefore? Because material characteristics are not in fact material characteristics. Everything with form is unreal; if all forms are seen as unreal, the Tathâgata is seen." This last statement, "if all forms are seen as unreal, the Tathâgata is seen," is the key. What does it mean to see all forms as unreal? We must know for ourselves that form is emptiness. One way to do this is to see into a koan.

With his question Subhuti is also asking how we can recognize an awakened person. How can we know for sure that someone is awakened? A story is told of a messenger who was ordered by the emperor to find a certain Zen master. The messenger searched high and low until one day he came to a village. "Yes," said one villager, "I know where the man you are looking for lives." "Where is that?" cried the messenger. "Under the bridge with the beggars." "Under the bridge with the beggars! How will I ever recognize him?" "Oh that is easy. Take some melons with you and offer them. The one who seizes the melon is the master. He loves them."

When we try to find special marks or characteristics in ourselves or in others, we separate ourselves from what is. We attempt to order our perceptions and actions according to some preconceived ideal, or we judge another according to this ideal. It is precisely this living by rules, images, and ideals that causes us to go astray. To be awakened we must let go of all images and ideas about awakening. Dogen says that the awakened person does not know that he, or she, is awakened. This has the same meaning as Joshu's "When I am hungry I eat; when I am tired I sleep." God does not know he is God. But we must not forget the irony.

Transcending the Teaching

My teaching of the good law is to be likened unto a raft. The dharma must be relinquished; how much more so adharma.

This is the statement to which I referred at the beginning of this book, which indicates the provisional nature of Buddha's teaching. It is in the nature of language to impose an absolute on what is essentially relative and impermanent. This is the value of language; it gives stability to experience. In my book *The Butterfly's Dream* I gave the following example to help make this point clear. Suppose there is a stain on the wall. You are aware of it at some level, but you do not take note of it. Then suppose you focus your attention on the stain and give it a name. Let's call it Joe. Every time you come into the room, you will see Joe. The stain has acquired a quality of permanence that it did not have before. This does not mean that before you named it it just appeared and disappeared; rather, the stain emerged from and then blended again with the total situation. When it blends it does not stick out. After it has been named it cannot blend in quite the same way. Furthermore, if after it has been named the stain is removed, one can ask, "Where did it go?"

So we can see that language, while giving stability, has side effects; it causes what was essentially alive and flowing to become deadened and fixed. This fixed, dead quality is what gives us the feeling that we live in an alien land, from which something vital is missing. This is the theme of many of the legends of the Holy Grail. Unless we are very careful, Buddha's teaching, too, will contribute to our illusions; it, too, will stifle and kill. The teaching of Buddha is a teaching not of the truth, but of a way to the truth. It is like putting up scaffolding so that a house may be built. When the house is complete, the scaffold is torn down. To be able to recover original nature, we must break the spell of language. When we have crossed the bitter ocean of life and death, we leave behind the raft. This is similar to the saying of Christ, "Know the truth, and the truth will make you free." Truth in this case is not fixed and frozen in a formula, but life-giving and free.

The sutra says,

> Do not say that the Tathâgata conceives the idea: I must set forth a teaching. For if anyone says that the Tathâgata sets forth a teaching he really slanders Buddha and is unable to explain what I teach.

Buddha also asks, "Has the Tathâgata a teaching to enunciate?" And Subhuti answers:

> "As I understand Buddha's meaning there is no formulation of truth called consummation of incomparable awakening. Moreover the Tathâgata has no formulated teaching to enunciate.

Wherefore? Because the Tathâgata has said that truth is uncontainable and inexpressible. It neither is nor is it not."

These sections give further examples of the contradictory nature of the teaching, which, as Subhuti says, is no teaching. One may well ask, "Is not the *Diamond Sutra* itself a record of the teaching of Buddha?" How can we reconcile this fact with Buddha saying, "If you say I have a teaching to give, you slander me"? If the sutra is not a record of the teaching of Buddha, then what is it?

This question is reminiscent of koan 11 in the *Hekiganroku*, in which Hyakujo scolds his students for being "mash eaters." Mash is what is left over after grapes have been crushed and the juice taken out; it has no nutritional value. He says, "Don't you know that throughout all of China there is not a single teacher of Zen?" The monks had spent their summer going around listening to talks about Zen. These talks, Hyakujo says, are mash. One of the monks steps forward and asks, "But are you not a teacher of Zen?" We search for awakening, and we search for a teaching that will bring us to awakening. Yet nothing needs to be done: awakening is letting go of the seeking; it has no connection at all with anything that we have ever been taught or have learned. Sadly, this is often confused with "doing nothing." "There is nothing that needs to be done" is not at all the same as "do nothing."

You read a book written by a spiritual person. As you read it you say, "This is right, this is just how it is. This is a good book!" How do you know "This is right"? How do you recognize the truth of what is being said? All that words, and therefore teachers, can do is to reflect back to you your own light. Thoughts are like dust motes floating in a sunbeam. The brilliance of the mote, the little shining rainbow that it carries, is simply the reflection of the light of the sunbeam. The dust mote itself has no light. In the same way thoughts—stimulated by sutras, or testaments, or teachers—are brilliant and true because they are the reflections of your own brilliance, your own truth. A question often asked in koans is "Why did

Bodhidharma come from the West?" My teacher Yasutani roshi said, "If Bodhidharma brought anything at all with him, he would not be worth a cent." What is there to teach? Who is there to teach? Who is there to learn?

No Wisdom to Attain

Buddha also asks Subhuti, "Has the Tathâgata attained the consummation of incomparable awakening?" and Subhuti says, "No."

"Consummation of incomparable awakening" could be said to be the goal of Buddhist practice. How then can Subhuti say that Buddha has not attained awakening? "Awakening" suggests something final, absolute. The idea of "attaining" suggests that one goes from a state of deficiency to a state of fulfillment. Awakening, however, is beyond all conception and can be neither final nor temporary. As I have just said, absolutes are imposed by language. We must see through the "stopping power" of words to be free from them, and this includes words such as *awakening* and *enlightenment*.

The awakened state and the unawakened state are not the same. Those in an unawakened state believe that something must be done, that something can be found, and that a teaching is available to help us find it. In the awakened state we realize that all beings are Buddha, so nothing needs to be done. Although there is no connection between teaching and awakening, teaching can bring our attention to this truth and so prepare us for the leap beyond thought, beyond all teaching. A monk said to a brother monk, "I went to my teacher with nothing and came away with nothing." The brother monk asked, "Then why did you go to your teacher?" The first monk replied, "How else would I have known that I went to my teacher with nothing and came away with nothing?"

Not only this, a teaching can help us to challenge our fixed assumptions, above all the fixed assumptions that we must have a teacher and that awakening is necessary. When the monk asks Joshu, "Does the dog have a Buddha nature?" he is asking about the awakened state. Joshu says, "No!" There is no awakened state. What is the meaning of Joshu's "No!" which applies equally to questions such as "Is the Tathâgata awakened?" "Does the Tathâgata have a teaching?" But the question remains, "What did Joshu have in mind when he said, "No!"? From the monk's point of view, this is like looking around at midnight for the light of day; from Joshu's, it is like looking around at noon for the darkness of night.

Through the genius of words I can convey to your mind what is in my mind. You could ask me, "What is in your mind?" and I could reply, "I was thinking that it looks as if it is going to rain, and I was wondering whether we should go out after all." Or I could say, "$E = mc^2$" or whatever. What I am doing is conveying to your mind some, or all, of what I have in my mind. So let me repeat the question. What did Joshu have in his mind when he said, "No!"? When one can see what this question is pointing to, then Subhuti's reply to Buddha's question "Has the Tathâgata attained the consummation of incomparable awakening?" will give no difficulty.

Think the Unthinkable

Therefore, Subhuti, the Bodhisattva, the great being, should produce a thought of utmost, right, and perfect enlightenment. Unsupported by form should a thought be produced; unsupported by sounds, smells, tastes, touchables, or mind objects should a thought be produced; unsupported by dharmas should a thought be produced; unsupported by anything should a thought be produced. A Bodhisattva should arouse the mind without resting it upon anything.

This is one of the Buddha's most famous sayings: "Arouse the mind without resting it upon anything." Earlier I pointed out that the word *prajna* means "arousing" or "heightening knowing." It means arousing the mind without resting it upon anything. It means releasing knowing from the sheaths of knowledge in which knowing is embedded.

But Buddha also says that the bodhisattva should produce a *thought* of utmost, right, and perfect enlightenment. What sort of thought could this be? We are told constantly to go beyond thought, and it is said repeatedly that thoughts make the prison in which we languish. Yet Buddha says we must produce a thought of perfect enlightenment! He goes on to say that this thought must not be "supported" by anything at all. In other words, it is not a normal thought, but it is still a thought. One of the most frequent questions I am asked is, "How does one arouse the mind without resting it upon anything?" Buddha gives the answer when he says that one should produce a thought unsupported by dharmas, unsupported by anything.

When we think, we always think about *something*. What is important to us is the "something" we are thinking about, the content of our thought. The content of our thought is the idea that it contains, as well as its accompanying feelings, sensations, intentions, and so on. Thinking about my home, or my family, or my job is always accompanied by feelings, sensations, intentions, and so on. It is also colored by "I," "me," and "my." All of this is the content of the thought. But when Buddha uses the word *thought* here, he does not simply mean an intellectual concept. He says that we must produce a *thought* that is not supported by anything at all. In other words, we must produce a thought without content. What kind of thought would that be? On another occasion Dogen said that one must *think the unthinkable*, which is the same thing. When we work with a koan such as "The Sound of One Hand Clapping" or "Who am I?" we are working with a thought, but a thought without content. We are arousing the mind, but not resting it upon anything; the mind is intensely active, just as the mind of a composer or writer or painter is intensely active, but active without content. What this means in effect is that one who works on a koan is an artist without an art.

The World is Not a World

The Tathâgata declares that a world is not really a world; it is called "a world."

One could equally well say, "An apple is not an apple, that is why it is called an apple." Or, more formally, "A is not A, which is why we call it A." This is quite different from the classical logic of the West, which says, "An apple is an apple" or, more formally, "A = A," or everything equals itself. A master said: "If you say you have a stick, I will give you one. If you say you do not have a stick, I will take it from you." What is an apple? What is a stick? Our problem is that we take the word for the reality.

If anyone listens to this discourse in faith with a pure lucid mind, he will thereupon conceive an idea of fundamental reality. We should know that such a one establishes the most remarkable virtue. World-honored one, such an idea of fundamental reality is not, in fact, a distinctive idea; therefore the Tathâgata teaches: "Idea of fundamental reality" is merely a name.

This is one of the more penetrating observations in the *Diamond Sutra*. When we have looked through the illusions that words create, we come to feel that we have reached bedrock, a fundamental reality, that from which all arises. But this belief in a fundamental reality still supposes a substratum, a resting place. Buddha's teaching is that no such substratum remains, not even the substratum of knowing, or being. This is the ultimate thought without content. The alchemists used the symbol of the fountain to convey a similar realization.

Dread and Fear in Practice

If anyone listens to this discourse and is not filled with alarm or awe or dread, be it known that such a one is of remarkable achievement.

Of course for one to experience this fear, one must really *listen* to the *Diamond Sutra*, not only with one's ears, but with one's eyes, as well, with our 360 bones and 84,000 pores, as Mumon says in his commentary on the koan "Mu!" Only then would one be filled with alarm and dread. Fear, anxiety, dread, alarm—these form a barrier on the way that, for many people, is insuperable. The "turnover rate" at the Montreal Zen Center is very, very high. To use the words of the Bible, "Many are called, but few are chosen." Many people are just not ready to give the time, energy, and effort that the practice requires. For others, Zen practice is simply unsuitable. But for the rest, the main reason for leaving is that they encounter this barrier. They either run right into fear and dread or else have such strong intimations of its onset that they leave before the fear strikes. Some of this fear may be accounted for by old experiences being revived. But most of it has another origin; it is the fear of the loss of self. This is the fear the sutra is referring to.

Sometimes this fear is accompanied by an uncanny feeling and even horripilation (goose bumps). It is the sort of fear that one might experience meeting a ghost. One has a feeling of impending doom of an unspeakable kind. As Heidegger puts it, "Dread strikes us dumb . . . all affirmation fails in the face of it. The fact that when we are caught in the uncanniness of dread we often try to break the empty silence by words spoken at random only proves the presence of Nothing."[1] This Nothing is the ultimate threat to the sense of self.

This feeling that the self is threatened occurs frequently during our lives. The threat may be physical, such as a lion in the wild or a mugger in the dark. But more often it is triggered by an idea.

One has a pain, and has the idea of cancer; one hears that a lot of people are being laid off at work, and one has the idea of being among them; one's lover seems distant, and one has the idea that she is about to leave. In each case, the sense of "I" is threatened.

We need this sense of "I," or self, because we need to be *something*. This is the basic motivation of a human being. Not only must I be something, but I must be a unique, distinct, special something. However, it is obvious I am not, at present, unique, distinct, special; hence, the satisfaction of this need for the sense of self is projected into the future—is going to be attained, realized, known, and so on. Moreover, other people to some extent sustain the sense of self. They tell us what we are, and what we can be. If I am a policeman, doctor, or teacher, it is because others have agreed to treat me as such. I determine whether I am a good policeman, doctor, or teacher by the reactions of others.

One hears people saying, "I don't care what other people think." This is absurd because, to a large degree, I *am* what other people think, I *am* what other people see. This is why most of us are so gullible, so conformist. Other people are the mirror in which we see, and create, the self. I am a collection of thoughts, ideas, and memories, with their associated feelings, all of which are mirrored back to me by others. When others—or even one other, if that person has a special significance for me—turn away from me, my sense of self is diminished and I am anxious. Among the worst punishments that can be inflicted upon someone is solitary confinement, in which the mirror is forcibly withdrawn.

Furthermore, the senses provide me with a steady flow of sensations, which are sufficiently similar to give the appearance of stability and permanence. All this is gathered around a central focus, something like iron filings around a magnet. This focus itself is a reflection. It is the reflection of the wholeness, which intrinsically I am. Each is whole, the whole, the One. This whole is without form or qualities of any kind. It is dynamism. We are constantly trying to grasp by naming this wholeness, and it is this wholeness that impels us with the feeling of uniqueness. When this sense of uniqueness is mirrored back to me, I am happy; when it is denied, I am sad.

A Greek myth tells of Narcissus, who was so in love with his reflection in the lake that he tried to embrace it, fell into the lake, and drowned. Each of us is Narcissus; each of us is trying to embrace the reflection of our own wholeness in an experience of uniqueness. The mirror in which we see our reflection is the awareness of other people. Death we perceive as the destruction of the mirror, the total annihilation of the sense of self, and this is the ultimate terror.

However, the threat to the sense of self can also arise from within, and it is this to which the sutra is referring. Christ, too, says that we must lose this sense of self, that we must allow it to fall into the ground and die.[2] But this death can hardly be free from fear and anxiety. The relation of the sense of self to wholeness is similar to the relation of a candle to the sun. Before the sun rises, a candle throws a lot of light, but as the sun rises, the light of the candle fades. Wholeness has the tendency to reabsorb the reflected self, just as, with the incoming tide, the sea reabsorbs the pools left behind when the tide receded. The reflected self is, as it were, swallowed. This feeling of being swallowed is common among those who experience this anxiety during Zen practice. This threat of being engulfed was once thought to be possession by evil spirits, and many religions have rituals and ceremonies to protect participants against the invasion of such malignant forces. For instance, magicians had such a ritual, in which they drew around themselves a circle that would be impervious to the threatening forces.

When we truly hear the *Diamond Sutra*, when we realize that even the idea of a fundamental reality is an illusion, it is as though the incoming tide washes over us. It is as though the self is about to be engulfed in a bottomless abyss, as though the light of our life is about to be extinguished. As the *Diamond Sutra* says, whoever is not anguished at such a moment, whoever does not pass through the dark night of the soul, living his own Gethsemane, is truly remarkable.

"No wisdom can we get hold of, no highest perfection,"

This avowal, that no wisdom can be obtained, is a strange one in a sutra dedicated to wisdom or prajna. But, again, the sutra is ensuring that we will not make *something* of prajna, that we will not commit the fallacy of misplaced concreteness. It is the same with perfection. I have just said that our need for a sense of self has an intrinsic quality: the need to be unique. This need to be unique leads us to seek the highest perfection. It is what we call idealism. The need to participate in some ideal state, some utopian realm, also plays a great part in the religious experience of people, so much so that the ideals of beauty, truth, and goodness often are confused with the holy. When all of these become intermingled with the search for our uniqueness and become subservient to it, bigotry, intolerance, and dogmatism enter. But, as the sutra says, no wisdom, no perfection can be attained.

Love Thine Enemies

One who is run down by others has hurt others in former lives, and this condemns him or her to fall into difficulties; but because others in the present lifetime insult him or run him down behind his back, the offenses in the former life are wiped out.[3]

Normally, when others run us down we turn upon them angrily and reply in kind. This response brings about more bad feelings, and so on. Most often, we feel that we are being attacked unjustly and have the right, if not the moral obligation, to defend ourselves. However, the *Diamond Sutra* says that we are not being attacked; we are being given the opportunity to pay our debts, debts we may not have any idea we have incurred. But this repayment is possible only if we have a teaching such as the *Diamond Sutra* and have truly seen that the bodhisattva has no sense of I or ego.

It is painful to be reviled, but this pain is possible only because we want to assert our uniqueness. All aggressive activity has, as an essential element, the assertion of self at the expense of others. When we assert ourselves, it is as though we are trying to set up a false center and demand that the world revolve around that center. We attempt to cajole, force, seduce, persuade, and blackmail others into complying with this false center. While we are successful in this charade we feel happy, successful, popular. We feel we are getting somewhere. But every now and then someone will refuse to read the lines we have given them, and we feel hurt, dealt with unjustly, put upon. We try to increase our persuasive power, try to force the center back into place. This can lead to a constant struggle with another or others, a struggle that often is accompanied by anxiety, stress, hostility.

If, however, we can recognize that a true bodhisattva has no I or ego, then we can release our hold on the false center and allow situations and events to find their own equilibrium. The immediate result can be a feeling of acute humiliation, which arises when we relinquish our claim to be unique. But when we stay with this feeling, the false center slips away. This is paying our debt. Think of Christ's injunction to turn the other cheek. This is the same as the injunction found in the *Diamond Sutra*.

True Self Is No-Self

It is impossible to retain past mind, impossible to hold on to present mind, and impossible to grasp future mind.

In the *Mumonkan,* koan number 28 tells of a Buddhist monk, Tokusan, who lived in the northern part of China. Tokusan was an ardent student of the *Diamond Sutra.* He lectured extensively on it and gave many commentaries upon it. One day, he heard that in the south of China a Buddhist sect called Ch'an[4] was teaching that it is possible for a human being to realize Buddhahood in this lifetime. He was incensed by this and was determined to prove the teaching heretical. He set off to do battle with the Ch'an teachers. He walked for many hundreds of miles, carrying his bundles of commentaries all the way. As he got to the South, and near to the territory of the enemy, he happened to stop at a teahouse for some tea and cookies, the latter having the quaint name of mind-refreshers.

The teahouse was run by an old woman, and Tokusan's bundle of books and notes immediately caught her eye. After he sat down and called for tea and mind-refreshers, the old woman, pointing to the pile of books, asked, "What are they?" "They are commentaries on a Buddhist sutra called the *Diamond Sutra*," said Tokusan. He probably said this with some condescension. "Oh!" said the old woman.

Then, after a pause, she said, "If you can answer me a question about the *Diamond Sutra*, I will give you the tea and cookies free of charge. But if you can't, you'll have to go on your way without them." "If I can't answer your question!" exclaimed Tokusan. "What do you mean, if I can't answer your question? Don't you realize that I am a teacher of the sutra, that I have expounded it to all kinds of monks and priests? Don't be foolish. Bring me the tea and cookies. How could you possibly ask me a question I can't answer?" "Nevertheless, Your Honor, will you not let a foolish old woman have her way for one question?" "Oh, alright," huffed Tokusan. "What is your question?" The old woman drew closer to Tokusan and, bending forward, said, "The *Diamond Sutra* declares that it is impossible to retain past mind, impossible to hold on to present mind, and impossible to grasp future mind." "Yes," said Tokusan, "I know that. I have lectured on it many times." "In that case, sir, which mind are you going to refresh with these cookies?"

Tokusan was floored! He just did not know how to answer. In desperation, he asked if a Zen master lived near.

If the *Diamond Sutra* is correct, if it is true that "it is impossible to retain past mind, impossible to hold on to present mind, and

impossible to grasp future mind," what mind, reader, are you using to read this page?

No Merit

Through the consummation of incomparable enlightenment I acquired not the least thing; wherefore it is called "consummation of incomparable enlightenment."

In the workshops I give to beginners at the Montreal Zen Center, I often recount the story of Emperor Wu's encounter with Bodhidharma. Bodhidharma, you may recall, was the founder of the Ch'an sect in China. He went to China in the fifth century and visited Emperor Wu. The emperor asked Bodhidharma, "I have done much for the development of Buddhism, have had monasteries built, have had the scriptures translated, have supported monks and nuns. Now, please tell me, what is the merit for all of that?" And Bodhidharma said, "No merit at all!" In the workshop, I point out that the emperor's attitude reflects the way most people think: I do good, should I not therefore go to heaven? In many religions there is even a celestial bookkeeper who adds the good points, deducts the bad points, and determines whether one is a candidate for heaven or hell, or will be reborn as a fox or an angel.

To bring home what Bodhidharma was saying when he declared "No merit!" I point out that, sooner or later, after the workshop participants have sat in meditation for a week, a month, perhaps even six months, they are going to ask, "What am I getting out of this? What is the merit for practicing like this?" Not infrequently, people will come to private instruction (*dokusan*) and complain, "I do not seem to be getting anywhere!" Often what they mean is, "I do not seem to be getting anything in reward for all the hard work I've been doing."

But what do you give to someone who has everything? A millionaire is poor because he has only a million dollars, whereas he could have the whole world. Nothing needs to be done. Before even one step has been taken, the journey is complete. Awakening is coming to see that no awakening is possible, and so putting down at last the grinding burden of desire, longing, regret, hope, and despair. Bodhidharma's "No merit!" is the proclamation of utter freedom. Buddha's "I acquired not the least thing" also is utter freedom.

Who Are You?

Though the common people accept the sense of self as real, the Tathâgata declares that the sense of self is not different from no-self. Those to whom the Tathâgata referred as common people are not really common people, such is merely a name.

I have said that others are the mirror in which we see the reflection of ourselves and, in this way, become certain that we are something. But who are others? Who are you? Everyone has the sense of self; everyone, at the same time, says, "You are," and so recognizes the sense of self in others. It is like the front and back of a picture: You are the front; I am the back, or I am the front; you are the back. But what are you? Let us put the question in a different form: How do I know that the person sitting in front of me is real, real as a "you"? I might reply to this question, "I hear you speak." By that I would mean not that I hear your body speak, or see your lips move and so hear a noise, but I hear *you*. Who is this "you"? What is this sense of self I call "you"? Something much more is involved than just what I see and hear, than just your body or your voice.

No doubt you are familiar with the internal monologue, or "infernal" monologue, as one person called it. A voice goes on without ceasing in your mind, a voice that argues, cajoles, explains, sometimes begs, often asserts. If you are attentive, you will see that often the monologue is actually a dialogue. Suppose I have something unpleasant I feel I must say to you. Before meeting with you, I will rehearse it in my mind just as though you were present, as though your sense of self were with me. You come into the room, and I say what I had been rehearsing, just as I rehearsed it, with the same feelings. You leave the room, yet I continue the conversation with "you." Who, then, are you? Are you but a creation of my mind? This cannot be. But then why does it seem that I talk to you when you are not here? Others are not others; "others" is just a name. You are not you; "you" is just a name. But, then, what are you?

> Who sees me by form,
> Who seeks me in sound,
> Perverted are his footsteps upon the way;
> For he cannot perceive the Tathâgata.

How many really can understand what is involved in these few lines? I, you, others cannot be seen by form. I cannot hear you, even though I hear your voice. I cannot perceive you, nor can you perceive me. I cannot even perceive myself. This inability to grasp oneself as a reality has always been a problem for philosophers and scientists, and, as a consequence, "I" has been relegated by some to just a ghost in the machine, or even an unnecessary postulate. "You say you are, then prove it," demands the positivist, the one who believes that only what can be weighed or measured, perceived or conceived, is real. This is the question that killed God. If it is real, it must have some effect, it must leave some trace, it must be capable of being seen or heard, if only as an echo, if only as a scratch on a photographic plate.

Scientists use the phrase *operational definition*,[5] by which they mean that words—and these include words such as *I, you, me*—must relate to something concrete. But Buddha says that you cannot see me by form, nor can you look for me in sound. Form, let us remember, includes feelings, thoughts, decisions, and consciousness, as well as objects. On the face of it, the problem of saying what I am, what you are, seems unresolvable. But, then, if we look around, the question becomes, How can you operationally define anything?

Let us start with something very simple: How would you operationally define the color red?[26] That is easy, a scientist would say. Red is a certain wavelength in the electromagnetic field, and this wavelength can be measured by a spectrograph. But, alas! What we are defining in this way is a wavelength, not the color red.

To see what I mean, let us ask, How would you operationally define the color red for a blind man? You could talk to him about wavelengths and so on, and he could well understand what you are talking about. But how do you make the leap from the conception of wavelength to the perception of red? Or how would you define the taste of a lemon to someone who had lost her taste buds? How would you define love to someone who had never loved? Or let's get right home and ask, What does it feel like to be you? Not you as a body, or you as a personality, but *you*. Red, yellow, green, the smell of a rose, the taste of chocolate, the feeling of warmth, the love in a smile—these we know, they are incontrovertible, but none of them can be defined operationally or any other way.

Coming and Going We Never Leave Home

If anyone should say that the Tathâgata comes, goes, sits, or reclines, he fails to understand my teaching, because Tathâgata has neither whence nor whither, therefore is he called Tathâgata.

One of the favorite questions of Zen masters is, "Where are you from?" In koan 15 of the *Mumonkan*, Tozan, who at the time of the koan was a wandering monk but who later became a famous Zen master, calls upon Ummon's temple. Ummon asks him, "Where are you from?" Tozan replies, "From Sato." Sato was the name of the last monastery Tozan had visited. Ummon then asks, "Where were you during the summer?" "Well, I was at the monastery of Hozu, south of the lake." "When did you leave there?" Ummon asks. "On September the first." And with that Ummon explodes and kicks Tozan out of his temple.

To go from "here" to "there," I must be *something* that is relative to here and there. I must be in space. If I come and go at a given time, I must be in time. It is precisely this idea of being a relative thing, one among many, bound in space and time, that the *Diamond Sutra*, and all Zen training, is trying to rid us of.

The Map Is Not the Territory

Words cannot explain the real nature of a cosmos. Only common people fettered with desire make use of this arbitrary method.

Not only do we want to *be* something, we also want to *know* something. This is true not only of intellectuals, but of us all. Storytellers, bards, minstrels, itinerant monks, and scholars always held a special place in society because, by passing on myths and legends, they gave us a reason for being someone, somewhere, and for some particular reason. What is now made available by television, film, the internet, books, what goes under the names of science, religion, philosophy, literature—those modern fountains of knowledge that come from our desire to bind time, to transcend space, to find meaning and purpose—once came from the mouths of wise men and women. We have always wanted to know, to grasp it all in some great plan, a living whole, a cosmos. We wanted to know this living cosmos because we are this cosmos, but are forever outside it, hammering to get in. It is a great moment when we realize that we do not have to be something to know, or know something to be, and can lay down the burden of purpose, reason, and goals.

Thus shall you think of all this fleeting world:
A star at dawn, a bubble in a stream;
A flash of lightning in a summer cloud,
A flickering lamp, a phantom and a dream.

A haiku says the same thing, slightly differently:

An old pond —
A frog jumps in,
Plop!

1. Martin Heidegger, *Existence and Being*, (Chicago: Henry Regnery, Gateway, 1949).

2. "If anyone wishes to go my way, let him deny himself and take up his cross and follow me. He who tries to save his life will lose it; but he who loses his life for my sake will save it." Truly truly, I say to you, unless a grain of wheat falls into the earth and dies, it remains alone; but if it dies it bears much fruit. The one who loves his life loses it and he who turns aside from life in this world shall keep it for eternal life."

3. This section forms the basis of koan 97 in the *Hekiganroku*. I have commented on this koan at length in *To Know Yourself* (Rutland, Vermont: Charles E. Tuttle) pp. 217-232. See that book for a further discussion of this section of the sutra.

4. The word *ch'an* is a Chinese alliteration of the Sanskrit word *dhyana*, meaning "samadhi" and "meditation." The Japanese and the Chinese use the same characters when writing, but pronounce them differently. Hence, "Zen" in Japanese is "Ch'an" in Chinese.

5. "The operational meaning of a term (word or symbol) is given by a semantical rule relating the term to some *concrete* process, object, or event, or to a class of such processes, objects, or events" (my emphasis). *Dictionary of Philosophy*, edited by Dagobert Runes (Lanham, Maryland: Littlefield, Adams).

6. This question was raised by no other than P. W. Bridgman, the Nobel Prize winner who introduced the notion of operational definitions.

CHAPTER 5

THE *VIMALAKIRTI SUTRA*

How heal the phantom body of its phantom ill,
Which started in the womb?
Unless you pluck medicine from the Bodhi-tree,
the sense of karma will kill you.

The *Vimalakirti Sutra*, which is in the Prajnaparamita tradition, came into being about the time of the birth of Christ. Its basic teaching is that of the *Prajnaparamita Hridaya*: form is emptiness, emptiness form. Robert Thurman, in the introduction to his translation of the sutra, which I will use in this chapter, says that the equation of form with emptiness does not mean that form does not exist. It is, instead, a qualification of what the concept "form" means. Thus, the expression "form is emptiness" is not a statement of nihilism and does not do away with matter, but, instead, does away with the notion that form is absolute, having its own independent existence. Although one can agree with this as far as it goes, the expression "form is emptiness; emptiness is form," is much more radical than simply a qualification of what the concept "form" means. To appreciate the radical nature of this expression, a turnaround in the very nature of knowing is necessary.

The Hinayana School believes that human beings are full of impurities; impurities that come from thoughts, which in turn create negative emotions and passions, which in turn lead people into suffering. Because of the suffering, more negative emotions are generated, creating more suffering, so a vicious cycle is set up. The vicious cycle eventually becomes a dwindling spiral. According to this school of thought, it is necessary to purify ourselves by passing through a hierarchy of stages until we come to the point where we need to live only one more life, after which we will become Buddha. As Buddha, one enters Nirvana and will not return to earthly existence again.

This is very similar to the Roman Catholic view of life, which holds that we are born in sin, but, by behaving correctly, by being obedient to the teachings of Christ, the Church, and the Pope, we will eventually become angels in a heavenly realm. Both the Catholic and the Hinayana traditions teach that we are impure, that we must purify ourselves, and that we can enter a more perfect realm beyond the earthly one as a reward for purification. In essence, they both say that an impure state exists in contrast to a pure state. Furthermore, the higher realm has an independent existence; heaven exists in parallel with the earth. Sometimes a more sophisticated explanation is offered, in which, instead of two parallel existences, a lower and a higher consciousness, or a lower and a higher self are involved, the higher self having to purify itself of the impurities of the lower.

In contrast, the Mahayana view is that this very earth is heaven, and our bodily existence is Nirvana. As Zen Master Hakuin says in his verse *In Praise of Zazen*, "This earth where we stand is the pure lotus land, and this very body the body of Buddha." This is sometimes expressed as "Nirvana is Samsara, Samsara, Nirvana," which is ultimately a variation of the formulation, "Form is emptiness; emptiness is form." Our problem, therefore, is not one of purification, but of waking up beyond all opposites to our essential purity. This understanding lies at the heart of the *Vimalakirti Sutra*.

Lay Practice

The *Vimalakirti Sutra* shows the spiritual virtues of lay practice. Vimalakirti was a deeply awakened layman who lived at the time of

Buddha. His awakening, and the wisdom and compassion that flowed from it, it was said, far exceeded that of all the bodhisattvas. One of the themes of the sutra is that practice within lay life—with its full responsibilities of job, family, and social commitments—can lead to deep awakening.

The tone of the sutra is established by what Vimalakirti says in this passage:

Noble sir, flowers like the lotus, the water lily, and the moon lily do not grow on the dry ground in the desert, they grow in the swamps in mud. In the same way, the Buddha qualities do not grow in living beings who are already awakened, but in those living beings that are like swamps and mud of negative emotions.

In a similar way, a seed does not grow in the sky, but on the earth. So the Buddha qualities do not grow in those who are already saints, but in those who seek awakening after having built a mountain of egoistic views as high as Mount Everest.

Noble sir, by the same token, one can understand that the family of the Tathâgatas includes all our passions. For example, noble sir, without going out into the great ocean it is impossible to find precious, priceless pearls. Likewise, without going into the ocean of passions one cannot reach the mind of pure knowing.

When they consider the mess that their lives are in, when they look inside themselves and see the slushing and oozing of anger, bitterness, disappointment, and lust, many people ask, "What hope is there for me? I have an aspiration for a spiritual life, yet here I am wallowing around in all these negative emotions." Vimalakirti says that awakening is possible precisely because of these negative emotions. Everyday mind, that is the way.

The first and essential step on the way is to wake up to the realization that life really is confusing, that it contains much ugliness, that we have often betrayed our higher feelings, that, as Buddha said in the first noble truth, life is suffering. When we become open to this, it is a great moment, but one that is often accompanied by deep despair.

On Practice

Vimalakirti had this to say about practice:

> Friends, the body of the Tathâgata is the Dharmakaya[1] born of knowing. The body of a Tathâgata is born of the stores of merit and wisdom. It is born of discipline, of practice, of prajna, of awakening and of the perfection of awakening. It is born of love and compassion, joy and impartiality. It is born of charity, perseverance and self-control. It is born of gentleness and patience. It is born of the roots of virtue planted by constant effort. It is born of concentration, insight, meditation and absorption. It is born of learning, wisdom and ways of liberation. It is born of truth. It is born of reality. It is born of pure awareness.
>
> Friends, the body of the Tathâgata is born of innumerable good works. You should turn your aspirations toward such a body and, in order to eliminate the sicknesses of the passions of all living beings, you should arouse the wish for unexcelled, perfect enlightenment.

One of the things Vimalakirti is saying in this passage is that awakening by itself is not enough. For example, he says that the body of the Dharma is born of awakening and the perfection of awakening. In other words, after awakening more work remains to be done to perfect the awakening. People sometimes come to awakening spontaneously, without having practiced in a tradition. They may feel that they have arrived and need do no further work. But awakening does not do away with our habitual reactions. Awakening brings with it considerable freedom, and if this is directed not to the eradication of past ways of reacting, but to their enhancement, inflation can result. If, as so often happens, one who has done no further work starts to teach, the result can be disastrous.

By contrast, Vimalakirti says, "You should arouse the wish for unexcelled, perfect enlightenment." He is saying that we must not engage in false modesty, protesting that we will be satisfied with just a glimpse of the truth, but must be open to the wholeness and completeness that we inherently are. But if we do arouse this wish, we must be prepared to pay the price, which is, as T. S. Eliot said, "not less than everything."

Humor

This sutra was called by Buddha "the reconciliation of the opposites," the opposites of purity and impurity, heaven and earth, form and emptiness, something and nothing. It is one of the most immediately accessible of the sutras and is full of wry humor. The first part of the book tells of Buddha trying to persuade one or another of his disciples to go to Vimalakirti and ask after his health, but each of them backs off. All have had an experience in which Vimalakirti has corrected their understanding in such a devastating way that Buddha's disciples knew that, as soon as they went near him again, they would run into problems. So when Buddha says, "You go and visit Vimalakirti!" one after the other says, "No, not me! Please find someone else."

Eventually, Manjusri is persuaded to visit Vimalakirti, and the sutra says, "Thus eight thousand Bodhisattvas, five hundred disciples, a great number of Sakras, Brahmas, Lokapalas, and many hundreds of thousands of gods and goddesses, all followed the crown prince Manjusri to listen to the Dharma. Vimalakirti, in anticipation of such a crowd, said to himself, 'Manjusri, the crown prince, is coming with numerous attendants. Now may this house be transformed into emptiness.' Then magically the house became empty. *Even the doorkeeper vanished* [my italics]."

Thereupon, the venerable Sariputra, the fall guy in the sutra, has this thought: "This house does not have even a single chair. Where are these disciples going to sit?" Vimalakirti, who could read his thoughts, says, "Venerable Sariputra, did you come for the sake of the Dharma or did you come for the sake of a chair?"

Later, during the intense discussion between the bodhisattvas and Vimalakirti, Sariputra thinks to himself, "If these great Bodhisattvas don't adjourn before noontime, when are they going to eat?" Vimalakirti chides him once again, saying, "Reverend Sariputra, the Tathâgata has taught the eight liberations. You should concentrate upon those liberations, listening to the Dharma with a mind free of preoccupations with material things. Just wait a minute, and you will eat food as you have never before tasted."

Vimalakirti's Sickness

The fundamental theme of this sutra is Vimalakirti's sickness, and the disciples' struggle in the face of Buddha's request that one of them go to visit him. For many people the idea that a spiritual person could fall sick is terrible. They believe sickness shows that spirituality is lacking. I once gave a friend a copy of the book by Shunryu Suzuki, *Zen Mind, Beginner's Mind*. But after a short while she returned it, saying that she did not want to read it. When asked, "What's the matter? Why don't you want to read it?" she replied, "Well, he died of cancer. How can anybody of any spiritual level die of cancer? Why didn't he cure himself?" People even ask sometimes whether an awakened person feels pain!

Ironically, Vimalakirti has something very similar to say. At one time Buddha fell sick and asked Ananda to get some milk for him. Ananda took the begging bowl and went to the house of a great Brahman family. Vimalakirti came to the door and asked him what he was doing there with his bowl in his hand so early in the morning. Ananda replied that the body of the Lord was sick and needed some milk, and he had come to get some.

Vimalakirti then said, "Reverend Ananda, you must not say such a thing. The body of the Tathâgata is as tough as a diamond because he has got rid of all the instinctual traces of evil, and is just filled with goodness. How could disease or discomfort affect such a body? Reverend Ananda, be quiet and do not put the Lord down. Do not say this kind of thing to others. It would not be good for the powerful gods or for the Bodhisattvas coming from the various Buddha fields to hear you say this kind of thing. Reverend Ananda, a world ruler who has only gone a short way in his practice is free of disease. How then could the Lord who has the highest level of attainment have any disease? It is impossible."

When Ananda heard this he said to himself, "Have I misunderstood what the Buddha asked me to get?" He was then very upset and ashamed. But then he heard a voice from the sky, "Ananda, what the householder says is so. Nevertheless, since the Buddha has appeared during these dark times, he uses this skillful means of being an ordinary person to teach others. Please get the milk!"

Vimalakirti's view of sickness is a departure from the usual Zen view, and one wonders why this passage appears in this sutra, particularly because the sutra says that Vimalakirti himself has fallen sick. After all, as Zen Master Rinzai said, "Followers of the Way, if you say that Buddha is the ultimate, how is it that after eighty years of life he lay down on his side between the twin sala trees and died? Where is Buddha now? It is clear that like us he lived and died and so is not different from us."

Buddha did, of course, die. He died of old age. As he said just before his death, "I have now grown old, and full of years, my journey is drawing to its close, I have reached the sum of my days, I am turning eighty years of age; and just as a worn-out carriage can be kept going only with bits of rope, so the body of the Tathâgata can only be kept going by bandaging it up." Furthermore, many other spiritual teachers have died of cancer: Shenryu Suzuki, Ramana Maharshi, Ramakrishna, Nisargadatta, and Katagiri roshi all died of cancer.

In koan 3 of the *Hekiganroku*, Master Basho is seriously ill and about to die. A monk comes to pay his respects and asks Basho, "How do you feel?" Basho replies, "Sunfaced Buddha, moon-faced

Buddha." A sun-faced Buddha lived for a very long time, a moon faced Buddha lived for but a short time. We cannot assess, our well-being on the basis of how we are feeling, or our depth of spiritual perception on whether we fall sick or not.

Buddha wanted somebody to visit Vimalakirti to see how he was doing. In his disciples' protests about why they do not want to visit Vimalakirti, the teaching of the sutra unfolds.

Sariputra: Ordinary Mind

The first disciple Buddha approaches is Sariputra. He says, "Sariputra, go and ask after the health of Vimalakirti." And Sariputra says,

> Lord, I do not want to go to ask Vimalakirti about his health. Why? I remember one day I was sitting under a tree in the forest, absorbed in contemplation, when Vimalakirti came to the tree and declared, "Sariputra, you should not be absorbed in contemplation like this. You should absorb yourself in zazen in such a way that neither body nor mind appears anywhere in the three worlds, in such a way that you are a completely ordinary person, without letting go of stillness. You should do so in such a way that you perform your day-to-day activities without losing awareness, in such a way that you can be an ordinary person without letting go of your spiritual development. You should practice in such a way that the mind neither settles within nor moves toward outer things; in such a way that you can do whatever is necessary without becoming attached to anything in particular; in such a way that you are liberated without giving up the passions that are the province of the world."

What Vimalakirti is saying is that one should not try to evade the dust and turmoil of our ordinary, everyday life in order to practice. His instruction is very much like what Nansen said to Joshu: "Everyday mind is the way".

But Vimalakirti seems to contradict Nansen when he says, "You should absorb yourself in zazen so that neither body nor mind appears anywhere in the three worlds." The three worlds make up everyday mind. They are the world of desires, wishes, judgments, and intentions; the world of things and ideas, of forms and theories, and, finally, the world of no-form, what we sometimes call "nothing" and "nowhere." However, Vimalakirti does not mean that you should practice in such a way that the body and the mind just disappear and you are suspended in space. He means that the feeling "I am the body" and the feeling "I am the mind" drop away. Furthermore, when he says that you should practice in such a way that the body and mind do not appear anywhere in the three worlds, you do not need to be afraid that you will vanish. He goes on, "You should absorb yourself in contemplation in such a way that you can manifest the nature of an ordinary person without abandoning your spiritual nature."

This, of course, is what the Mahayana revolution is about and also what this sutra is emphasizing. Vimalakirti is challenging Sariputra to go beyond the belief that he is something in the world of somethings, and to do this without leaving the world of somethings.

Vimalakirti goes on to say, "You should absorb yourself in contemplation so the mind neither settles within nor moves outward to external forms." In other words, a spiritual life does not abide "in here" and a mundane world lie "out there." This is why one should not give up the present situation, as Sariputra had obviously done, to search for a situation more favorable to one's spiritual welfare. Where you are is the best place for your spiritual welfare. There is not one place for spirituality and another for earning your living. They are one and the same place.

Vimalakirti says further, "You should absorb yourself in contemplation in such a way that the thirty-seven aids to awakening are manifest without turning towards any convictions." The thirty-seven aids are the Hinayana aids for achieving purity. Vimalakirti says that these all manifest automatically. One does not have to have a special belief or religion. One does not have to be a Buddhist, Christian, Hindu, or whatever. When he says, "without any deviation toward conviction," he means that a spiritual life, a life that leads toward realizing one's wholeness and completeness, is natural to a human being. The problem is precisely that we are obstructing this realization with our convictions.

Maudgalyana: The Teaching of No-Teaching

The next bodhisattva to whom Buddha appeals is Maudgalyana. Vimalakirti had chided Maudgalyana when he found him teaching the Hinayana view of the Dharma to a group of laymen, giving them the precepts to ensure their rebirth in heaven. The Hinayana teaching assumes an entity to be saved, and Vimalakirti said one should not teach this, but should teach the truth.

Maudgalyana was one of Buddha's chief disciples and was reputed to have miraculous powers. He was no doubt teaching from the Hinayana viewpoint because he felt this was all that laypeople could accept. Vimalakirti says that this is not so, and that they should be taught the ineffable Dharma. He says, furthermore, that the Dharma is without qualities or distinguishing characteristics, and he gave a long list of characteristics the Dharma does not have, all of which undercut the idea of *something*. He rejected the idea that we must purify ourselves, and he rejected the idea that there is a self that has to be saved.

The Dharma, he says, is without living beings, because it is free from the illusion of living beings. In other words, as Buddha said in the *Diamond Sutra*, one should vow to save all sentient beings, knowing no sentient beings exist that can be saved. The Dharma is free from the notion of self because it is free from desire. It is free from the idea of being alive because it is beyond birth and death. It is without personality because it is not dependent upon memory or upon future goals.

He goes on to say that the Dharma is not something in itself, it is not some specific teaching, for example, because it is free from words and letters, so therefore cannot even be expressed, and so transcends any movement of the mind. It is surely this that gives us the greatest difficulty. The mind only ever knows *something*; what does not have a form cannot be grasped by the mind and so cannot be known. Things arise because the mind moves. If knowing something is a movement of mind, how can the mind itself be known?

However, because the Dharma has no form and cannot be grasped, we must not conclude that it is nothing, nonexistent. Vimalakirti says, on the contrary, that the Dharma is omnipresent, because it is like vast space. We can be misled by this simile, particularly when it is used with the metaphor of "emptiness." Vast space suggests that the Dharma is infinitely extensive, so this simile can reinforce the tendency to "look" outward for the Dharma, for the true self. But the Dharma is said to be like vast space because it is unobstructing. Nonobstruction is the feature that space and the Dharma share.

Vimalakirti says the Dharma, which for the moment we could call knowing, permeates evenly throughout all things, because all things are included within it, nothing is outside. This, it could be said, is what is meant in Buddhism by *omniscience*. Nothing lies outside knowing, and, with omniscience, fundamentally all things are known without discrimination, judgment, or evaluation. He says the Dharma, or knowing, conforms to reality by the process of nonconformity. This means that knowing follows all the contours of existence without clinging to any. Bankei said the same, but more concretely. "While you are facing me, listening to me speak like this, if a crow cawed, or a sparrow chirped, or some other sound occurred somewhere behind you, you would have no difficulty knowing it was a sparrow or crow, or whatever, even without giving a thought to listening to it, because you were listening by means of the Unborn," by which he means that knowing is always knowing and cannot be other than knowing. It comes from nothing else, and does not change into something else, it is always the same, it never appears or disappears.

The Dharma, what Bankei was calling the Unborn, what Joshu's "Mu!" refers to, and what we have called knowing, is immovable, because it is independent of the six objects of sense. Things move only relative to other things. If the mind is dependent upon things, then movement becomes inevitable. When one sees the world from the standpoint of emptiness, then not only does the mind not move, but nothing else moves either. This is why Vimalakirti says that the Dharma is without coming and going, for it abides nowhere. Its true nature is emptiness, and without any distinguishing marks. It is beyond consciousness and transcends the scope of eye, ear, nose, tongue, body-mind, and thought. It is neither high nor low. In other words, nothing can be said, or thought, about the Dharma. It is inconceivable.

Vimalakirti then asks a question that reverberates throughout the Zen tradition: "How can one teach anything about such a Dharma?" This is a question broached by a number of the koans, including, for example, koan 13 of the *Mumonkan*, in which Zen Master Tokusan and two of his disciples, Ganto and Seppo, play out a drama around this question. In koan 27 also, a monk asks Nansen if there can be a teaching that the ancients never taught. Nansen replies, "Yes, there can be." But what is it? Nansen says it is not mind, nor Buddha, nor things. But what kind of teaching is this? It does not lie in the words, even though Nansen conveys it by words.[2] In koan 11 of the *Hekiganroku*, Zen Master Hyaku-jo chastises his monks for visiting the monasteries of China listening to masters talk about the Dharma. He says that the monks are a lot of mash eaters, that is, they are going around consuming what is left over after the juice has been crushed out of grapes. He says, "Don't you know that throughout China not a single teacher of Zen can be found?"

Vimalakirti says that even the expression "to teach the Dharma" is too much. He says further, "When one realizes that no words are adequate, then no teacher of Zen is possible, no one to listen to Zen, and no one to understand it. Talking about the Dharma is like a dream person talking to dream people."

But then Vimalakirti delivers the same paradox Buddha delivered in the *Diamond Sutra*: You must teach the Dharma even though it is unteachable. He says that Maudgalyana should be sensitive to people's spiritual capabilities. Using his intuition, with deep compassion, and out of gratitude to Buddha, Maudgalyana should have a pure intent and, from the deepest part of himself, teach the Dharma in order that the three treasures—Buddha, Dharma, and Sangha—may be preserved.

Mahakatyayana: What Is Impermanence?

Buddha then takes his request to Mahakyshapa, Subhuti, and Purna, but all of them refuse to go. He tries Mahakatyayana, but he refuses, as well. He says that on one occasion he had given a talk on impermanence, suffering, selflessness, and peace—*anicca*, *dukkha*, *anatman*, and *Nirvana*. Vimalakirti came and said that one must not talk about ultimate reality as though it were engaged in activity, and as though it were involved in creation and destruction. The real meaning of impermanence, or *anicca*, is that no thing is created or destroyed. One must see, by realizing the emptiness of the five skandhas, that one is not born. This is what suffering, or *dukkha*, means. The self and not-self are not opposed; this is what selflessness, *anatman*, means. That which is not something cannot burn, and that which is not burning cannot be extinguished. This absence of extinction is what *Nirvana* means.

When Vimalakirti says that the real meaning of impermanence is that no thing is created or destroyed, one is at first taken aback. Yet if things could be created, things would have to come from nothing into something; and if they could be destroyed, they would have to go from something to nothing. This would imply that both the nothing from which something derives and the something that is derived are permanent, even if the something is temporary. Vimalakirti's impermanence does away with both of these concepts.

Upali: No Absolution from Sins

Let us consider one more disciple. Buddha then goes to Upali and asks him to visit Vimalakirti. Upali says he does not want to go either. He says that on one occasion two monks told him they had committed a sin but were too ashamed to confess this to Buddha. They asked Upali to absolve them of their sins. Upali said he was talking to them about this when Vimalakirti came to say, "Do not aggravate further the sins of these two monks by absolving them." This differs widely from the Roman Catholic view, wherein confessing one's sins and receiving absolution are essential. The teaching of the Mahayana is that one cannot be absolved from one's karma. This does not mean that one does not confess one's sins—the Zen tradition has its own ceremony for this—but confession is a way to *pay* one's debt; one does not confess to be *absolved from* the debt. In any case, it is axiomatic in Buddhism that one cannot be absolved by another. It is stated:

> By oneself evil is done
> By oneself one suffers
> By oneself evil is undone
> No one can purify another.

The Mahayana attitude differs here from the Hinayana attitude, wherein samadhi absolves one from one's karma and is a way of burning up karma. According to the Mahayana, not even awakening can absolve us from our karma. This causes a great deal of perplexity. What is the point of practicing if we have nevertheless to live out our karma?

It is not easy to answer this question. A very important koan, the second koan of the *Mumonkan*, is concerned with just this matter. A monk asks a teacher, "Is the awakened man free from the law of cause and effect or not?" Is a man free from his karma when he comes to awakening? The teacher says, "Yes, he is freed from his karma when he comes to awakening." For that reply he has to live out, as retribution, a karmic existence of five hundred lives as a fox. The teacher was deeply awakened—so why does his karma compel him to live five hundred lives as a fox for saying that a deeply awakened man is not subject to the law of cause and effect? Vimalakirti gives the answer when he says, "Reverend Upali, sin is not to be found within the mind, outside the mind, or between the two. Buddha has said that living beings are afflicted by the scourge of thought, and they are purified by the purification of thought." The problem, in other words, is not to give the right answer, it is to get beyond all answers.

When we are in pain, we naturally seek a way out of pain. When we perceive that the pain comes from past actions and thoughts, we seek an action, penance, or prayer that will enable us to find a way out of the painful karma. But all of these actions, penances, and prayers simply turn the wheel of Samsara. The scourge of thought, Vimalakirti tells us, afflicts us. Our actions, penances, and prayers are themselves afflictions of thought. As long as we believe in "something," consequences of that belief will arise. Those consequences will create their own consequences. Thus arises what we could call a continuity of cause and effect. Everything emerges from everything else, and everything returns into itself again. Yasutani roshi used to say, "When the conditions and circumstances are right, then things appear."

Now what are these "things" that appear when causes and conditions are right? This is really the issue. It is not whether I can stop or change the consequences that appear from, and give rise to, these things. As long as I believe I have things, as long as I believe I have a body, a mind, thoughts, then consequences are going to arise from them, and they in turn will be subject to causes and conditions. We cannot escape or be absolved from that.

Vimalakirti then asks, "Reverend Upali, the nature of the mind by virtue of which your mind is liberated, does it ever become impure?"

The "nature of the mind" by virtue of which your mind is liberated is emptiness, and emptiness cannot become impure, or mixed with thoughts, feelings, or sensations. It is like a mirror, which cannot be scratched by a sword it is reflecting, or burned by a fire it reflects, no matter how sharp the sword or how fierce the fire. A scholar asks Nansen to talk about Zen. Master Nansen asks in return, "Can that cloud in the sky be pinned to the sky?" What can we pin our karma to? To what is karma attached that gives it its power? Karma is simply attached to karma. It is karma that gives karma its power. It is things that give things their power. As long as there are things, there is karma. As long as there are things, karma has power. Therefore, as long as we seek ways by which we can absolve ourselves and others of the consequences of things, we are pinning those people inevitably to their karma. By his very absolution, a priest locks the person confessing into the karmic prison of cause and effect.

Vimalakirti says that purity of mind is the ultimate nonexistence of thought and imagination, and that the absence of a self is the intrinsic nature of the mind. No thing is created, destroyed, or endures; things are like magical illusions, clouds, and lightning; all things are evanescent, not remaining even for an instant; they are like a dream, a hallucination, and delusion; they are like the moon in water, and like a reflection in a mirror.

The Visit to Vimalakirti

Eventually, the bodhisattvas decide that they will all go to visit Vimalakirti, there being safety in numbers. And "eight thousand bodhisattvas, five hundred disciples, a great number of Sakras, Brahmas, Lokapalas, and many hundreds of thousands of gods and goddesses, all followed the crown prince Manjusri to listen to the

Dharma." Vimalakirti sees Manjusri coming, and a most remarkable dialogue follows. It is very subtle and requires all one's attention as the two move between different levels of discourse.

Vimalakirti says, "Manjusri, welcome, Manjusri! You are very welcome. There you are without any coming. You appear without any seeing. You are heard without any hearing."

This is the beginning of a dharma duel. We must ask ourselves, What does Vimalakirti mean when he says, "There you are without any coming. You appear without any seeing. You are heard without any hearing"?

When I was young I once attended a vaudeville show in which a magician made a young woman appear and disappear onstage. It was only later that I realized this had been done by carefully placed mirrors, which were disguised so that one was unaware they were there. When the mirrors were turned slightly, the woman appeared and when they were turned back to their original position, she disappeared. The audience, therefore, never actually saw the woman; they saw only her reflection in the mirror.

At the time, I did not doubt for a moment that I was seeing the woman. If one had a big enough mirror, one could reflect a whole city in it, and it would seem to anyone unaware of the mirror that the reflection was a real city. Very often when children start looking at mirrors, they get the feeling that the reflections are real and try to see what is on the other side of the mirror. Lewis Carroll took advantage of this in his book *Through the Looking Glass*.

In the same way, although we see the world reflected in the Great Mirror of Samadhi, we see it as real, as something having its own being. Just as a reflection is totally dependent on the mirror for any reality it has, the world around us only gets its reality from the reality that we are.

The world is suspended in reality, and that reality I have called the Mirror Samadhi. The mirror does not go anywhere. It is the reflections in the mirror that move. Just as things are reflections in the mirror, the sense "I am something" is a reflection. As Nisargadatta said, the painter is part of the painting. Because of this, there is no seeing, because there is no seer; there is no hearing, because there is no hearer.

Manjusri replies, "Householder, it is as you say. In the end who comes, comes not. Who goes, goes not. Why? Who comes is not known to come. Who goes is not known to go. Who appears is finally not to be seen."

Who comes, who goes, who appears? This Mirror Samadhi is not a cold abstraction. Emptiness conjures up a coldness that is almost arctic. Yet all the warmth, the compassion, the wisdom, all that is living, comes out of, or, better still, is intrinsic to, this Mirror Samadhi. This is why many religions have personified it, turning it into a being. In Mahayana Buddhism the notion of bodhisattva arose because it retains the sense of the warmth and life of personhood. This is the advantage of personification.

But to make emptiness into a being tends to make it appear to exist apart, with me here and God there. An enormous gulf now seems to yawn between that being and me. That being is independent of me, and I have to relate to it, and this will push us back into the clash and clang of individual, separate existences. In order to avoid these kinds of problems, we must not forget that words like *emptiness* and *God, Being,* and *Self* are only expedient means, fingers pointing to the moon.

We need not be afraid of emptiness. It is not an extinction of anything. We lose nothing in coming to awakening except our illusions. Although awakening is often referred to as a death, it is the death of what separates us from ourselves and gives us pain. It is the death of death. Everything is fulfilled in awakening. Things do not lose their contours and become blurred. On the contrary, everything stands out as perfect. Even a cracked cup, said Yasutani, is perfect. It is almost as though a light shines from within everything, because one is looking at things now without a curtain of expectation, demand, opinion, and tension obscuring it.

"I Am Sick Because the Whole World Is Sick."

Manjusri goes on to inquire about Vimalakirti's health and then asks, "Householder, where does your sickness come from? How long will it last and how is it at the moment?"

Vimalakirti replies, "Were all living beings free of sickness, the Bodhisattva would also be free of sickness." Another way of saying this is, "I am sick because the whole world is sick."

Because one is human, one suffers. At first one suffers on one's own account, and when this suffering has been alleviated, when a self is no longer involved in the sickness, then one can carry the burden of others. One is burdened not so much by the suffering of this or that individual person as by the fact of suffering itself, above all by the fact of useless suffering, what I have called elsewhere "donkey suffering." Useless suffering afflicts most people. Some, however, are able to turn the suffering around, to realize that it is the expression of the human condition and, further, that to free themselves from suffering they must free themselves from the belief that they are *something*. When they realize this, suffering, instead of being an obstacle, becomes an ally.

The Emptiness of Emptiness

Manjusri then asks, "Householder, why is your home empty? Why have you no servants?"

We must make a distinction here between an empty house and the emptiness that the *Prajnaparamita Hridaya* refers to when it says that "form is empty." It is like someone asking, "What is in the drawer?" and receiving the reply, "Nothing is in the drawer; it is empty." Vimalakirti's house has been emptied. It has neither furniture nor even a doorkeeper. But this is not the emptiness of the *Prajnaparamita*.

Vimalakirti turns the dialogue around and says, "All Buddha fields are empty." A Buddha field, we could say, is a universe. Each of us has a Buddha field. This is the totality of experience that is possible for us. We do not live in *the* world, we live in *a* world, although we perceive it, and can only perceive it, as *the* world. It is obvious that the world of a Japanese peasant of the eighth century and the world of a person living in Montreal in the twentieth century are not the same. Indeed, in a way, we cannot even say that they are different; they are incomparable. It is as someone said: everything is unique; there is no difference. We talk, for example, about "the Second World War" as though only one war took place, but as many Second World Wars occurred as there were people affected. Each of these people felt that what he or she was engaged in was *the* war. Someone might protest, "But the fact that all these people interpreted the war differently does not mean that no single, overriding world war occurred." But who knew this overriding war, or where or how was this totality, called the world war, contained? In God's mind? But that would be simply God's world war, *another* world war and not *the* world war.

In a family of five, are five families. We tend to forget this; looking from a specific point of view, we perceive only one family. But this perception is not of the living family; it is an abstraction existing only in thought. The brothers and sisters, the mother and wife, the husband and father each has his or her own family. Each has a Buddha field, and, because it is *a* family and not *the* family, each Buddha field is empty.

All these Buddha fields come together because they are empty. It is the emptiness of the Buddha field that makes interpenetration completely possible, and it is this interpenetration that makes me feel that I perceive *the* world when I perceive *a* world.

The physicist tells us that we can look at the world as a hierarchy of forms: atoms, molecules, cells, organs, and bodies. From the point of view of physics, each of these levels is real. Molecules have properties that atoms do not have; cells have properties that molecules do not have, and so on up the hierarchy. Yet these levels are all interpenetrating. This is so because they are empty. It can be said that physics is not a study of the *world*; it is a *study* of the world. In other words, the mind and the world cannot be separated; form is emptiness, emptiness is form.

One way to illustrate this is to suppose for a moment that I have a glass of pure water. I let a drop of blue ink fall into the water. This ink now is suspended in the water and is inseparable from it. If we say that the pure water is emptiness and the blue ink is the form, or the pure water is the study, the blue ink the world, then we begin to appreciate what is being said here.

We are *a* world; we are not *part of the* world. You are not part of the whole; you are a whole.

Manjusri challenges Vimalakirti by asking, "What makes them empty?" What is it about a Buddha field, what is it about this world, that makes it empty? Why do we say it is empty? And Vimalakirti replies, "A Buddha field is empty because of emptiness."

Now, on the face of it that does not help us very much. But he is saying that it is in the nature of things that they are empty. When we hear this kind of statement—"A Buddha field is empty"—we often take what we think of as the world, that which we feel is real and of which we believe we are parts, and try to find some way we can agree that it is empty. In other words, we look at it from the point of view of all its complexity and apparent is-ness and there-ness and being-ness, and then we try to conceive of it as being empty. But as a result we are bound to say, "You know, when you talk about emptiness, I am completely confused."

The nature of the world is emptiness. We have to bypass all our convictions and opinions, our expectations and so on. We must stop pointing to something in the world and saying, "That is real." The very act of pointing, indeed, any act at all, is already the expression of emptiness. It is not that emptiness is an attribute of things. Emptiness is not a special property or quality things have, like weight, for example, or size.

Realizing this takes humility. Without humility, we cannot make the first step. And the realization must be far-reaching. First we must listen—not simply hear, but listen; and to do this we must let go of our prejudices, our preconceptions, and our cleverness. We must say to ourselves, "Perhaps something really important is being said that I just cannot afford to miss."

But let us return to the question "Why are things empty?" A Buddha field is empty because of emptiness. That is its nature. Things do not exist apart from emptiness.

Manjusri goes on to ask, "What is empty about emptiness?" In other words, How can I get a grasp on the emptiness of emptiness? Vimalakirti replies, "Constructions are empty because of emptiness." Manjusri asks, "Can emptiness be conceptually constructed?" "Even that concept is itself emptiness. Emptiness cannot construct emptiness."

In this dialogue, our minds are being pushed to the limit. The sutra is removing all possibility of form from emptiness.

The question is asked and then the question is taken away because the very words we use lack any self-nature; words, too, are empty. Many people when they encounter this kind of dialogue say, "I am confused. How can I get out of this confusion?" But that question, too, is empty; even the "I" that is confused is empty.

In pushing our minds to the limit, the sutra is showing us how to practice. When one asks the question "Who am I?" the tendency is to believe one is something and then go on to ask, "What kind of something am I?" One says to oneself at some level, "Well, obviously I am something, so what sort of something am I?" Everyone knows "I am something," just as everyone knows "The world is something." But this "something" is a cul-de-sac from which no exit is possible. Most people, after asking themselves this question for a while, say, "I'm confused," "This question is dry," "It doesn't mean anything to me," "The question doesn't seem to resonate," and so on. Of course it doesn't, because one is saying, "I know who or what I am. Why does he ask me this stupid kind of question and then expect me to sit and ask 'Who am I?' Why does he not give me something that I can really sink my teeth into?"

But do not take that first step! Even "Who?" already is too

much. One already is downstream once one asks "Who?" A whole metaphysics, a whole universe springs up from that seed "Who." "Who" already is a formulation, something, but, as Vimalakirti says, "Even that concept 'who' is itself empty. And emptiness cannot construct emptiness." In this question "Who am I?" the purpose of the word *who* is to encourage you to bring prajna to bear. More simply, the question is an invitation to arouse the mind without resting it upon anything. The questioning is the arousing, the arousing is emptiness. The questioning is not the formulation of a concept; the question is empty. One cannot rest upon anything. Another way of saying this is that it is not so much that one *has* a question but that one *questions*. One does not try to answer the question, but rather arouses the need to know.

The French author of *The Supreme Doctrine*, Hubert Benoit, said that when a fox wants to rid itself of fleas, it goes into the water backwards. As it does so, all the fleas hop up the body, along the head, and onto the fox's nose, until just the fox's nose sticks out of the water. Then the fox dips his nose under the water, and away go the fleas.

This is what is happening in this dialogue. The questioning is reduced to the minimum. If everything is empty, how can I even make this statement? Manjusri asks, "Householder, where should emptiness be sought?" Vimalakirti replies, "Emptiness should be sought among the sixty-two convictions you have." The sixty-two convictions are all our everyday opinions, expectations, knowing what I know, what everyone knows, and so on.

Words give the illusion of separate and distinct things. Logic, based as it is on the principle that everything is equal to itself (technically A is A), has to some extent been constructed to reinforce that illusion. Words are a self-defense mechanism, and they defend us against the abyss of ourselves without any support, ourselves as intrinsically empty. Our practice is to awaken the faith that we do not need support. Many religions have a god to support the faithful; secure in this support, their believers can let go of all other supports. This can give great freedom on the one hand, but bondage on the other. When we turn our responsibility over to someone else, we enjoy this kind of freedom. This is where dictators and demagogues get their power. In the same way, when some people say, "I've turned to Christ and am free," this freedom has been bought at a very high price—their spiritual heritage, their entire spiritual life. In cults, people turn themselves over to the leader, so the ambiguities, confusions, and doubts of everyday life are laid to rest. This gives a certain freedom. But should they break away from the cult, they will have to re-create their lives, pick up again the confusions, uncertainties, ambiguities; only then will they recognize the degree to which they have betrayed their spiritual trust. Their agony will be overwhelming.

But instead of turning over to this demagogue, or whatever it is, and so being supported just by that one holding idea, you could turn yourself over to having no holding idea, no world idea, no weltanschauung, no view. And in turning yourself over to no view or, as the sutra says, holding to nothing whatever, you cut that string which holds you to your world, holds you to your Buddha field. As the *Prajnaparamita Hridaya* says,

The Budhisaltra of Compassion, from the depths
    of prajna wisdom,
saw the emptiness of all five skandhas
and sundered the bonds of suffering.

The initial cut, the initial suspension or release from a view or viewpoint, from a world idea, holding idea, or whatever one may call it, may be brief. But however brief, however shallow, it banishes forever the illusion that one cannot live without support. Gone also is the belief that to be, one has to be dependent on the world. With that goes one's slavery. We are enslaved by the world because we feel that, in order to be, we are dependent on the world and its values. The world, we say, is real.

Manjusri then asks, "Where should the sixty-two convictions be sought?" "They should be sought in the liberation of the Tathâga-ta." The liberation of the Tathâgata is the freedom from binding ideas, beliefs, and convictions. It is seeing into the emptiness of no matter what thought, image, or form. We do not recognize that the room that we are sitting in is an idea. We believe the room we are sitting in is real, we believe it is *the* room. It is, however, our *idea* of a room, in just the same way that, if you see a face in an inkblot of the Rorschach test, the face is your idea of a face. Your idea of the world is your Buddha field. And everything is interdependent with-in your Buddha field. Everything holds everything else together and in place. It is this mutual support that makes it seem solid, gives it its convincing quality. But it also makes it vulnerable, because if you see through just one atom of dust in that world, the whole world will shake. It will lose its invincibility.

Then Manjusri asks a final question, "Where should the liber-ation of the Tathâgata be sought?" And Vimalakirti replies, "It should be sought in the primal mental activity of all beings." Now, the primal mental activity of all beings is the first arising of thought. A movement of the mind occurs, and out of this move-ment everything follows, and what are called *vasanas*, or mind waves, begin surging. The vasanas leave behind a residue that cre-ates the sense of continuity and duration. Vimalakirti says that one must see into this primal mental activity. A more direct way of say-ing this is, "Before the thought 'I am' arises, what are you?"

Consoling the Sick

Manjusri asks, "How should a Bodhisattva console another Bodhisattva who is sick?" A bodhisattva in this context is someone who is, and has been, working upon himself, or herself. One should also remember that, according to Buddhism, all human beings who have not seen into their true nature are sick. It is for this reason that Buddha has been called the Great Physician.

Vimalakirti begins by saying that one should remind the sick person that the body is impairment. In other words, one shifts the context within which the sick person views the sickness. As long as I see the body as the absolute, as the sine qua non of my existence, and consider the decay of the body, through age or sickness, as the decay of my very being, then all sickness is a calamity. But, being reminded that the body is an impairment, I can shift my perspective and see that the body is something that is happening to me, sickness is but another way in which the body happens, and as a happening it is passing, or changing, constantly.

Dwelling on the disgusting aspects of the body is sometimes recommended as a meditation procedure. But Vimalakirti says that we do not have to do this. Whether one prizes or rejects the body, it is in principle the same. In both cases we are attached to the body by judgments about it, through the belief that it is something enduring and real.

Vimalakirti says that one should remind the sick person that the body is the cause of misery but should not encourage him to find relief in liberation. We must recognize the first noble truth of Buddha, that life is suffering. By dwelling with that we begin to find the strength to release our grip. It is as the hymn of Jesus says, "If you knew how to suffer, you would have the power not to suffer."[3] To seek liberation from suffering is to deny that life is suffering; this search for liberation comes from the secret belief that the suffering is an accident, that it is not an intrinsic part of life. To see thoroughly into the truth that life is suffering is already liberation; it is liberation from all the suffering that we endure in our attempts to escape suffering.

One should remind the sick person that the body is without a self-entity, but, even so, living beings must be saved. One should also remind him that the body is without substance, but that he ought not to look for peace outside. He should be urged to confess his sins, but not so that he feels he does not have to bear their consequence. He should be encouraged to have compassion for all who suffer, knowing the meaning of suffering from his own experience, now and in the past. He should be encouraged not to give way to depression. He should but use the illness as another wa practice, to rid himself of the need to be something special, a the cravings this need generates. In this way he will be able truly to fulfill the first of the bodhisattva vows, to save all sentient beings.

Manjusri asks how the sick person should control his own mind. Vimalakirti says the sick person should say to himself, "Sickness comes from my taking the illusion for the real, and the real for an illusion. It comes from negative emotions that arise because of the way I understand things, because, in truth, nothing can be sick. While the body may be sick, the viruses nevertheless flourish. In other words, sickness comes from the belief '*I* am alive, *I* am involved.' The truth is I am not alive, 'I am' is life itself."

Vimalakirti goes on to say that the body is the outcome of four elements—earth, air, fire, and water—and in the elements one cannot find any owner or agent. As modern Westerners we would not say that the body is the outcome of the four elements, but we might want to remind ourselves that it is a very complicated collection of atoms or molecules. None of these, just like none of the four elements, has any owner or self. No self at all resides in the body, no "I," so, ultimately, no "I" that can be sick.

"I am" is not something. "I am" is the ultimate subjective. If one can see this, then one can let go of the belief that one is a personality. Furthermore, by examining carefully this idea that "I am something," one can come to realize that the body, at best, is a collection of things. In this case, when this collection is born, only things are born; when it dies, only things die. These things that make up the collection called a body have no awareness of or feeling for each other. When they are born they do not think, "I am born;" when they die they do not think, "I die."

Vimalakirti and Nonduality
The heart of this sutra is the dialogue between the bodhisattvas and Vimalakirti on the subject of nonduality. This dialogue, or at

ZEN & THE SUTRAS

least the part of it in which Vimalakirti gives his famous response
to the question "What is nonduality?" forms the basis of koan 84 in
the *Hekiganroku*.

In the introduction to this koan, a Zen master, Engo, says,
"Though you say, 'It is!' 'it is' cannot affirm anything. Though you
say, 'It is not!' 'is not' cannot negate anything. When 'is' and 'is not'
are gone beyond, then getting and losing drop away. All is open
and unobstructed. Now I want to ask you, What is in front of and
what is behind me? Some monk may come forward and say that
the Buddha hall and the temple gate are in the front, and the bed-
room and the sitting room are behind. Tell me, is that man open-
eyed? If you can see through him, I will acknowledge that you have
seen the ancient worthy."

This sets the theme of the dialogue between Vimalakirti and
the bodhisattvas very well. The dialogue opens with Vimalakirti
asking how one goes beyond duality, how one attains to emptiness.
Engo asks, "What lies beyond 'is' and 'is not,' What lies beyond 'in
front of' and 'behind'?" This question is reminiscent of a mondo
between Rinzai and a monk. The monk comes to Rinzai with the
intention of asking him some questions. He bows and is about to
speak when Rinzai strikes him. "Hey!" says the monk. "Why are
you hitting me? I haven't even opened my mouth yet." "What is
the good," growls Rinzai, "of waiting until you have opened your
mouth?"

How do you go beyond the opposites and so avoid Rinzai's
wrath?

All the bodhisattvas give their opinions: one says that we must
get beyond creation and destruction by seeing that nothing is created; another says that we must get beyond the idea of me and mine;
another says that we must see into the emptiness of defilement and
the opposites of purity and defilement will be no more; yet another
would have us let go of distraction so that it will not be necessary to
concentrate, and in this way the opposites of distraction and concentration will be no more. And so it goes on. This dialogue is

important because it gives us an opportunity to look at all the forms that the assumptions of something and nothing drive us into. But the responses of the bodhisattvas prepare us for the response of Vimalakirti. First of all, however, it is Manjusri's turn.

They ask Manjusri, "How do you get beyond 'is' and 'is not,' 'being' and 'nothing'?" Manjusri says that, although what the bodhisattvas have said is acceptable in itself, by giving an explanation they have already fallen into dualism. In this, Manjusri gives the reason for koan practice. In koan practice one cannot simply give explanations, one must demonstrate the truth, and one can do this only by realizing that one *is* the truth, and that truth means that no one is expressing the truth, and no truth needs to be expressed. Then, echoing the blow Rinzai gave to the monk in the story just recounted, Manjusri says, "To know that no one is teaching, to teach nothing, to say nothing, to explain nothing, to pronounce nothing, to point to nothing, to demonstrate nothing, that is the entrance to the principle of nonduality."

Then they all turn to Vimalakirti, and, in the words of koan 84 of the *Hekiganroku*, "Manjusri said to Vimalakirti, 'Each of us has had his say. Now I ask you, What is the Bodhisattva's gate to the One and Only?'"

The koan ends there.

Setcho, the compiler of the koans, adds a completely unnecessary question: "What did Vimalakirti say?" And then he says, "I have seen through him." In the sutra it says, "Thereupon Vimalakirti kept his silence, saying nothing at all." It is a pity that the sutra has to say this; the koan, without Setcho's comment, is much better.

What kind of silence is Vimalakirti's silence? In the sutra one often comes across the expression "The Bodhisattva was struck dumb [by Vimalakirti's wisdom] and did not know what to say." It is obvious that Vimalakirti's silence was not the silence of dumbness. If one is silent because one does not know, it means that something can, after all, be known, and we are back in the dualism of something that can be known and a knower who can know it.

On other occasions, one hears of a guru, such as Sri Aurobindo, taking the vow of silence. This is a teaching silence. Even though he was silent as far as his lips were concerned, he was not silent; his mind was still very noisy, and he still wrote notes and books. His silence was a relative silence. Words cannot convey the truth, and so one does not use words, but instead uses silence to convey the truth. But silence does not convey the truth either. Another koan in the *Mumonkan* says that a non-Buddhist went to Buddha and said, "Please do not give me words and explanations, I know that these are useless. But please do not give me silence either, this is of no use to me at all. Now I beg you, what is the truth?" In the koan it says, "Buddha just sat there."

Another form of silence is sometimes given when a student comes for a private interview (dokusan). He may well be asked, "Where are you when a dog barks?" or some similar question. The student knows that if he tries to give any explanations he will be banished from the interview room. So sometimes he sits in silence. He is still banished. Why? The student is conveying something to me, the teacher. This something may be silence, but it remains something, a message.

Basically, in Zen practice one is taught, "Nothing needs to be done." The problem is that people do not realize how radical this nothing is that needs to be done. Just as Vimalakirti says that emptiness itself is empty, this nothing that needs to be done is, itself, nothing that needs to be done.

---

1. *Kaya* means "body," so *dharmakaya* means "the body of the Dharma."

2. I have commented at length on these koans in *The World: A Gateway* (Boston: Charles E. Tuttle, 1995).

3. G. R. S. Meade, *Hymn of Jesus* (London: John Watkins, 1963) translator.

CHAPTER 6

THE *LANKAVATARA SUTRA*

He who holds that emptiness
Is without form, that flowers are visions
Let him enter boldly!

The *Lankavatara Sutra* was taken to China by Bodhidharma, the
first Chinese patriarch of the Zen sect, and is one of the sutras particularly revered by Zen Buddhists. Bodhidharma said, "As I
observe, there are no other sutras in China but this; take it for your
guidance, and you will naturally save the world."[1] The word *Lankavatara* literally means "entering into Lanka," Lanka being one of
the islands off the south of India, where the sutra is said to have
been delivered by Buddha. The chief theme of this sutra is the
doctrine of self-realization or awakening.[2]

Among other things, this sutra sets out, in some detail, what
D. T. Suzuki calls Buddhist psychology. Our main interest in this
chapter will be in this aspect of the sutra. Suzuki points out that
this "psychological" emphasis, which is so distinctive of the *Lankavatara*, gives this sutra a unique position in Mahayana literature.[3]
Buddhism was intended not to be a theoretical study, but instead,
as I said at the beginning of this book, to be a practice. This also is
true of Buddhist psychology. To quote Suzuki, "Whatever psychology or logic or metaphysics it may contain, is to prove the main
doctrine,[4]" and the main doctrine is the possibility and nature of

awakening. In the sutra, Buddha says, "My teaching consists of the cessation of the suffering arising from the discrimination of the triple world; in the cessation of ignorance, desire, deed, and causality; and in the recognition that an objective world, like a vision, is the manifestation of mind itself."[5]

Although Suzuki uses the word *psychology*, this should not be interpreted the way we use the word in the West, where it means either an interpretation and analysis of the personality and its functioning or a purely theoretical discussion of the functions and aspects of human thought and behavior. The *Lankavatara* is interested in the personality, but only to show its illusory nature and how this illusion comes into being. Its main emphasis is on what consciousness means and how consciousness evolves through different modes, as well as the part "me" and "I" play in this evolution. It would, therefore, be more appropriate to call it a noology (that is, a study of the *nous*, or spirit) than a psychology. Although this sutra can be quite difficult to grasp, it should not be missed if one is interested in understanding the nature of mind that makes spiritual practice possible.

The *Lankavatara* would have been compiled by a practicing Zen master for people who were also practicing. The words in the sutra would therefore not simply have been defined by other words, but would have been pointers to direct experience. Because of this, familiarity with the dictionary meanings of these words is not enough, nor is a meaning acquired by familiarity. The meaning must be understood from *within* rather than from outside. This is quite different from the way one studies academic psychology. It will be important to ponder the *experienced meanings* of the key words. For example, to what does the word *I* refer? What is the felt or experienced difference between *I* and *me*? Do the words *awareness* and *consciousness* refer to the same thing? Zazen is the way to understand what working from within, rather than from outside, means. Thus, truly to understand this sutra, it is important to have an authentic practice.

About words and their meaning, the sutra says, "Words are subject to birth and death, meaning is not; words are dependent upon letters, meanings are not." It goes on to say,

> You should energetically discipline yourself to get at the meaning itself. The meaning alone is with itself and leads to Nirvana. Words are bound up with discrimination and lead to rebirth. Meaning is attained from much learning, and this much learning means to be conversant with meanings and not with words. To be conversant with meaning means to ascertain the view which is not at all associated with any philosophical school and which will keep not only yourself but others as well from falling into false views. Let seekers for meaning reverently approach those who are much learned in it, but those who are attached to words as being in accord with meaning, they are to be left to themselves and to be shunned by truth seekers."[6]

I remember talking with a university professor about words and their meanings. He belonged to the new school of thought which declares that words have no meaning. While this is true, meaning does sometimes have words.

Vijnana as Consciousness

According to the *Lankavatara Sutra*, consciousness, or *vijnana*, has eight "levels."[7] The first five of these are what, in the West, we call the five senses: the eye vijnana, the ear vijnana, and so on; the sixth is *manovijnana*, very roughly what we call intellect; the seventh level, which is unfamiliar to the West, is called *manas*; the eighth is the *Alayavijnana*, the "storehouse" vijnana—it is the consciousness in which the essence or, to use the Sanskrit word, *bija* of all experience is stored. The eighth is what we could call pure consciousness or *nonreflected knowing*, and in Sanskrit is known as *jnana*. As the sutra says, "What constitutes the Tathâgatas in essence as well as in body is jnana." In other Buddhist texts this level is further divided into an eighth and a ninth level. However, in this sutra these are combined into one level, which, as we shall see, is highly ambiguous.

The word *vijnana*, which I have translated as "consciousness," is made up of two words: *vi*, meaning "divided," and *jnana*, from the root word *jna,* meaning "basic awareness," knowing without content. Earlier, I referred to this root word when talking about prajna. The English word *consciousness* can be seen to point to a similar divided nature, as it, too, is made up of two words: *con* meaning "with" or "together with," and *scio*, meaning "to know." In other words, by etymology, the word *consciousness* could mean "to know together."

Each of the five senses has its consciousness. In the West we tend to overlook this and consider seeing, hearing, tasting, and so on, to be purely physical. "I see the flower" implies an eye, sense data flowing to it from the flower, and the flower. For most people, consciousness of the flower is either taken for granted or denied altogether. The positivists and behaviorists say that everything involved in seeing can be explained adequately without using the notion of consciousness. The *Lankavatara*, in contrast, by using the expression *eye vijnana*, insists upon consciousness as an essential element in the process of seeing. Indeed, it goes much further to say, "The world [as we see it] exists not; pluralities of things rise from the Mind being seen [externally]; body, property, and abode, are manifest to us as of the Alayavijnana."[8] "Mind only" is the basis of the *Lankavatara* teaching.

Let us now consider the term *Alayavijnana*.

Alayavijnana: The Different Modes of Awareness

Alaya is "pure awareness," "self-nature," or, as it is sometimes called, "Buddha nature." To understand what pure awareness means, we must make a distinction between *awareness* and *consciousness*. Think about the distinction between looking and seeing. Someone could well say, "I was looking right at it but did not see it." We make this kind of distinction, too, between hearing and listening. We hear all kinds of things, but listen to relatively few of them. If you live in the downtown area of a city, you hear the sounds of traffic all the time, but rarely do you listen to them, unless, for example, you are anxiously waiting for a friend to arrive by car.

In a similar way, I can say, "I was aware but not conscious," although it would be strange to say, "I was conscious but not aware." In other words, awareness is more basic than consciousness, which could be said to come out of awareness. I shall discuss in a moment what it means to say consciousness comes out of awareness.

Buddhist "psychology" makes this distinction between awareness and consciousness. "jna" is, as we have said, pure "awareness" or "pure knowing," and *vijnana* is "divided awareness," and so we could call it consciousness. Pure awareness, *Alaya*, also has two aspects and, before we can understand consciousness, we must come to terms with these aspects, also referred to as the eighth and ninth levels of consciousness.

The *Lankavatara Sutra* says that Alaya has two aspects: "the Alaya as it is in itself . . . and the Alaya as a mental representation." The Alaya itself is pure awareness; the Alaya as mental representation is a stage between pure awareness and consciousness. Pure awareness is constant and immutable; it is like space, and so, the sutra says, Alaya is also "known as the *incessant* because of its uninterrupted existence." But the sutra also says that Alaya is a representation. It is also manifested; that is, it is something that is happening, "because its activity can be perceived by the mind." Thus, the sutra says that Alaya is absolute in one respect but not absolute in another because as representation it is subject to evolution.[9] These two aspects of Alaya later came to be seen as two levels, but the *Lankavatara Sutra* sees them as two faces of an ambiguity. All of this is put succinctly in a mondo between a master and a disciple. It occurred while they were hoeing a field. The disciple asked the master, "What is it?" The master stood up, stuck the hoe in the ground, and stood there. The disciple said, "But, Master, you have the essence but not the function." The master asked in turn, "Then what is it?" The disciple went on hoeing.

Absolute Alaya

Alaya is our original nature, but within it lurks the incipient dualism between pure awareness, or jna—awareness without reflection—and the manifest aspect of Alaya, subject to evolution, which eventually will evolve into consciousness. Awareness without reflection corresponds to absolute Alaya, while "awareness of awareness" (what I shall call reflected awareness) corresponds to the manifest aspect. The culmination of Buddhist practice, according to the Zen tradition, is to awaken to the pure aspect of Alaya.

The first koan of the *Mumonkan*, "Mu!" the inquiry "Who am I?" and the koan "The Sound of One Hand Clapping" invite the practicer to awaken to the pure aspect of Alaya by "penetrating" directly into the absolute aspect of Alaya. This penetration is what is called in Japanese *kensho* or *satori* and in Sanskrit *paravritti*. Kensho is at the heart of Rinzai Zen practice, just as paravritti is at the heart of the *Lankavatara Sutra*, and this is brought out in the sutra's first chapter. This chapter tells of a man called Ravana, who is meditating alone. A moment earlier he was surrounded by Buddha and Buddha's disciples. The sutra says, "The entire assembly was seen on each mountain peak, and all the countries were present, and in each was a Leader." But then "the teacher and the sons of Buddha vanished away in the air leaving Ravana standing by himself in his mansion." Ravana asks himself, "How is this? What means this? and by whom was it heard? What was it that was seen? and by whom seen? Where is the city? and where is the Buddha?" He then asks, "Is it a dream then? or a vision? or is it a castle conjured up by the magicians? Is it dust in the eye, or a *fata morgana*, or a dream child of a barren woman, or the smoke of a fire wheel, that I saw here?"[10]

In this meditation, the stage is set for the rest of the sutra. Ravana's meditation also sets the stage for Zen practice, which basically comes out of the bewilderment that one feels in the face of a surrounding world. What is this world I see around me? Who is this me? When I say that I see the world, what is this seeing? The room I saw yesterday is not the same room I see today, nor is it the same room that was here ten years, twenty years ago. In a hundred years what will this room be? What will I be? Things do not change; change is things. Even as I look at the wall, it drifts into the past. The breakfast I ate this morning, it has already passed down the stream of time, and as I sit here, more and more events intervene between me and it, and inevitably it drifts away. My fiftieth birthday, thirtieth birthday, tenth, first birthday—nothing is stable or static. Where are these birthdays, these breakfasts, these walls that move down time? We say they are in the memory, but what is memory?

Ravana goes on, "There is neither seer nor seen, neither the speaker nor the spoken. If one sees things and takes them for reality, he does not see the Buddha. Even if one does not abide in the discriminating mind, one cannot see the Buddha." The first not-seeing means that in seeing things and taking them for reality we miss the whole, the unity. It is like when one sees iron filings arranged in the field of a magnet—one sees the filings but not the field.

But what is the meaning of the second not-seeing? "Even if one does not abide in the discriminating mind, one does not see the Buddha." Even if one does not take things to be the ultimate reality, one still does not see the whole. This is like Dogen saying that the awakened person does not know he is awakened. In Zen it is said, "Fire does not burn fire, the eye does not see itself." Even if one does not abide in the discriminating mind, one cannot see the Buddha because one is pure, *nonreflected* awareness, and so already Buddha.

Ravana was then "immediately awakened, knowing a turn-about in his mind and realizing that the world was nothing but his own mind." This realization is known in Zen as kensho, and, as we have already said, the whole thrust of the *Lankavatara Sutra* is what kensho is and how it is possible. The word used in the sutra for this turnabout is *paravritti*, which Suzuki translates, somewhat unfortunately, as "revulsion." He also talks of paravritti as a *catastrophic* experience and a *psychological* event, again misleading.

Revulsion arouses a negative feeling and is about as far as one can get from the true meaning of *paravritti*. I prefer to use the word *turnabout*. Another expression that could be used is the one I used earlier to translate the word Tathâgata: "to come to." One faints, or goes into a lowered state of consciousness, and then one "comes to." What is interesting about this expression, as I said before, is that one does not need to say what it is that one comes to.

Furthermore, paravritti is not an experience, so it cannot be a psychological event. One of the most famous of all Zen sayings is, "If you meet the Buddha, kill the Buddha!" Any experience—the experience of Christ, of Buddha, of cosmic consciousness, of light, of peace, of joy—is not it. A story is told about one of the Desert Fathers, to whom an angel of light appeared one day while he was meditating. The angel said, "I am the archangel Gabriel, and I have come to reward you for your devout life." The father replied, "Think again; you have come to the wrong person. I have done nothing to deserve reward." The angel of light disappeared, and the father continued with his meditation. This distinction between paravritti and experience is fundamental: no experience, no matter how striking or sublime, is awakening.

Experience, we could say, is *in* the mind, but the turnabout is *of* mind or, better, of knowing itself. The turnabout is from knowing *something* to *just* knowing; from knowing with content to knowing without content. It is not a psychological condition; this is why I am not happy with Suzuki saying that the *Lankavatara Sutra* is a psychological text. Psychology is concerned with the *forms* of the mind, that is, with the content of the mind and the relations of parts of this content to other parts. Paravritti is concerned with mind as knowing itself; paravritti is not extra, an acquisition after so much spiritual labor. As Suzuki says, "It is due to the Alaya's self purifying nature that a great catastrophe in it known as turning back occurs . . . the external world is no more adhered to as such, that is as reality; for it is no more than a mere reflection of the Alaya. The Alaya has been looking at itself in the manas' mirror."[11] Paravritti, in other words, is the natural culmination of the mind.

Manifest Alaya

Once again, we must recall that Alaya has two aspects: "the Alaya as it is in itself . . . and the Alaya as a mental representation." If we say Alaya is pure knowing, we have said only half the truth. The sutra says Alaya is "known as the *incessant* because of its uninterrupted existence [and] *manifested* because its activity can be perceived by the mind." It says Alaya is thus "absolute in one respect and subject to evolution in another."[12] In a moment we will look at the second aspect of Alaya, as mental representation subject to evolution. However, first, let us consider the troubling thought that, although Alaya is one as pure awareness, it seems to be two: pure awareness and evolving awareness.

Alaya: Not One, Not Two

In order to understand this difficult situation in which Alaya is one dynamic whole and yet two, let us remember the example of a mirror and its reflections. We could consider Alaya in its eternal mode as the mirror, and Alaya in its manifest, evolving mode as the reflections, which are constantly coming and going. The mirror is immutable, stable, "eternal," the reflections are always changing. Yet in practice we see the mirror and reflections as one undivided whole.

A favorite question of Zen masters is "Where are you from?" If I see myself as "a reflection," then I come and go, I am one reflection relative to all other reflections. But if I see myself as the mirror, coming or going does not apply—the mirror has no relation to any particular reflection; it is just one immutable whole. As Zen Master Hakuin says in his verse *In Praise of Zazen*, "Coming and going we never leave home."

A saying of Dogen's sums all this up. "Though not identical, they are not different; though not different, they are not one; though not one, they are not two." We shall come across the "one not two" concept repeatedly while discussing the *Lankavatara*.

Alaya and Memory

Alaya's manifest, evolving side sometimes is looked upon as a *storehouse*. Let us, for the moment, call this storehouse *memory*. Memory is not a "faculty" of awareness any more than water is a faculty of a stream. Just as water is a stream, memory is awareness.

Everything changes. This means that there is not the thing as it is now, the thing as it was, and the thing as it will be. Things do not change; *change is things*. Instead of three things—a past thing, a present thing, and a future thing—only change occurs. And without memory change would not be possible. If we can understand this, then we can understand why it is said in Zen that we are not born and do not die. To quote Suzuki again, "It is not that things are not born, but that they are not born of themselves, except when seen in the state of Samadhi —this is what is meant by 'all things are unborn.' To have no self nature is, from a more profound point of view, to be unborn. That all things are without self nature means that a constant and uninterrupted becoming continues unceasingly, a momentary change from one state of existence to another."[13]

Awareness is constant, unborn, but the content of awareness is never the same from one moment to the next. Now is always now.

We do not pass through a succession of nows, but the content of now is in constant flux. Nothing remains for a moment. You are born now, you die now, you have breakfast now, you go to bed now. It is sometimes said that one must be here and now. But there can be no "must" because one cannot be other than here and now. The mirror is constant, unborn; the reflections in the mirror are never the same from one moment to the next. Neither the content nor the reflections have self-nature. The reflections are manifestations of the mirror; the content of awareness is simply the manifestation of the unborn awareness. It is this change of content that we call memory.

I have said we are aware not of things, but of change, but, deeper yet, it is not so much that we are aware of change, but that we are aware of passing time. Furthermore, if we go to the very foundation, *awareness is passing time*. This is why we say that the content of "now" never remains. "Now" is awareness, and passing time gives rise to memory. This means that the present and the past can be seen not as two different times, but as two different modes of awareness. Change, when understood conceptually, is present/past/present/past/present . . . , but in terms of experience it is awareness/memory/awareness/memory. . . .

Our problem is that we try to understand time objectively, as something that happens to us and to things. This objective view of time is reinforced by clocks, and the movement of the earth and planets, stars and galaxies. Indeed, making time objective was one of humankind's earliest and greatest achievements, and was one of the discoveries that made consciousness possible. Because time was made objective, consciousness, as distinct from awareness, could stand outside time, and so exist apart from it. Unfortunately, although we tamed time in this way, we emptied it of significance, and now it has come to be an interval between two happenings, such as birth and death. At the same time that we create the stage for life, we create the possibility of death.

This means that time, when we understand it at a deeper level, is not "out there," not an abstraction, but the dynamic nature of true self. What we measure when we measure time is change of relationship between things, a change made possible by passing time, just as the passage of the wind makes possible the movement of the trees. Dogen said that Buddha nature is impermanent; this means that Buddha nature is dynamic. In Japanese, the "substance" of Buddha nature, what I have called pure awareness, is *ku*, or emptiness. Yasutani roshi said, "Ku is not mere emptiness. It is that which is living, dynamic, devoid of mass, unfixed, beyond individuality or personality—the matrix of all phenomena."[14] The nearest we can come to this in modern thought is the notion of a magnetic field. Even so, the field is an abstraction from life, Buddha nature is life itself.

Buddha nature is ku and, as memory, corresponds to what the *Lankavatara* calls the evolutionary nature of the manifest aspect of Alaya, an evolution made possible by the dynamic nature of ku. The sutra says the "Alayavijnana's function is to store up all the memory of one's thoughts, affections, desires and deeds."[15] I would like to be more precise; instead of saying Alayavijnana has the *function* of storing up memories, we should say that storing up memories is the very the nature of the manifest aspect of Alaya. In other words, we should not speak of two—Alaya and memory— Alaya *is* memory, memory *is* Alaya. Moreover, not only thoughts but feelings, desires, and so on, indeed, all that has occurred since beginningless time is stored in Alaya. In the words of Suzuki, "Memory [is] amassed in the Alaya since the beginningless past as latent cause." It is in this way that Alaya can be thought of as a storehouse. Indeed, Suzuki goes further: "The Alaya being super individual holds in it not only individual memory but all that has been experienced by sentient beings."[16]

What we must understand by this idea of Alaya as a storehouse is that memory, time, is cumulative. Dogen said, "Do not think that time merely flies away. Do not see flying away as the only function of time. If time merely flies away you would be separated from time."[17] Seen in this way, all that is—objects, organisms, civilizations, knowledge, and so on—is crystallized time. The past does not go away, but is the matrix out of which the present is made possible. It is like the design of a new car; it is made possible by, and comes out of, the designs of past cars, but at the same time it goes beyond them. I said that today's breakfast flows down the stream of time; but it does not flow away. It flows into the present as possibility. What is possible today is so by reason of what happened yesterday. This is quite obvious when we consider learning, growing, and evolution, but we seem to forget it when we think about memory or time passing. This cumulative nature of memory is what is called *karma*.

To support the notion that objects, organisms, civilizations, knowledge, and so on are crystallized time, the sutra says, "The material world, as well as the physical body, are manifestations of the mind known as Alayavijnana . . . [when they are] thus created they are seen in constant transmigration, they never remain even for a moment as they are, they flow like a stream, they change like a seed, they flicker like a candle light, they move like a wind or a cloud."[18] This constant transmigration is equivalent to the continuous flow of new forms, new crystallizations, coming out of accumulated memory, a flow made possible by the dynamic nature of Alaya.

In the same sentence, the sutra says that Alaya has "no active energy in itself; it never acts, it simply perceives, it is in this sense exactly like a mirror."[19] Let us try to see further into the apparent contradiction between saying "It has no active energy in itself; it never acts, it simply perceives," and Yasutani's saying, "it is that which is living, dynamic, devoid of mass, unfixed, beyond individuality or personality—the matrix of all phenomena."

"Awareness as" and "Awareness of"

We have seen within pure awareness a dualism that could be described as "awareness of" awareness. The sutra describes this by saying, "The Alaya *looks into itself* [my italics] where all the memory of the beginningless past is preserved in a way beyond consciousness and ready for further evolution."[20] These two—"awareness of" and "awareness"—are qualitatively different. To be more precise, we should call the first "awareness of" and the second "awareness as." Let us pause for a few moments to consider these two, then show how these considerations fit in with what the sutra is saying.

We talk about being aware *of* the world, aware *of* other people, aware *of* the flower, aware *of* the past, and so on. What is it, though, that we are aware of? Most people would say that we are aware of the world, but the sutra says that we are aware of "all the memory of the beginningless past . . . preserved in a way beyond consciousness and ready for further evolution." Another way of saying this is that what we are aware *of* is awareness as memory crystallized as objects. In other words, we are aware of awareness *as* the world, *as* other people, *as* the flower, *as* the past. Thus, when I say I am aware of the flower, this should, technically, be spelled out as I-am-aware-of-awareness-as-the-flower.

Because of what has been said in earlier chapters, we are familiar with the expression "form is emptiness." To say "form is emptiness" is not to say that emptiness and form are one and the same thing; it is to say that they cannot be separated. Emptiness is emptiness, form is form, yet form is emptiness. We can say that a flower is empty, but, taking into account what I have just been saying about things being crystallized awareness, we can also say that the flower is awareness. The flower is the flower, awareness is awareness, but the flower is awareness. This is but another way of using the metaphor of the mirror and the reflection. The flower is the reflection, the mirror is awareness. Yet, if you look around the room in which you are sitting at the moment, you will overlook this truth that the room is awareness. As Gurdjieff, the famous Armenian Greek teacher, said, "Man does not remember himself." You will forget yourself and just see the room. Yet the room is, as I have said, a reflection. When you look at the room, what you in fact see is not just the room, but the room as *reflection*; it is reflected in the mirror of awareness.

Because awareness is constant, because it has no defining characteristics, no qualities, it is overlooked. It is like the tenth person in the parable of the people crossing the river.[21] Because we overlook awareness, we see the room as "over there," as "objective," outside. A dualism seems to arise between the world that is seen and me, the seer. This dualism is illusory because it is simply brought into being by "awareness of." The dualism of "mind" and "matter" arises not because of two substances—a "world substance" and a "thinking substance," as the French philosopher Descartes would have us believe—but because of *two modalities of awareness*. If one can see into what is now being said, then, in a moment, the duality that has bedeviled humankind falls away. This falling away is kensho, paravritti. Parenthetically, the problem that has haunted Western philosophy from before Plato until the present time, the problem of what is a thing, also drops away.

I have already pointed out that *vijnana* means "divided awareness." I can now say that the two aspects in vijnana are "awareness of" and "awareness as." Another way of saying "you see" is to say "you are *aware of*." What you are aware of is the room reflected in the mirror of awareness. Another way of saying "reflected in the mirror of awareness" is to say that "you are aware of awareness as the room."

Alaya and Manas

So far, I have been referring to Alaya as pure awareness, which I have likened to a mirror, and Alaya as "awareness as," which I have likened to reflections. "Strictly speaking," says the sutra, "Alaya is not a vijnana."[22] That is to say, strictly speaking, Alaya is not consciousness. This, too, agrees with what I am saying, because "awareness as the room" is not consciousness. It corresponds in some way to what psychology refers to as the *preconscious* or *subconscious*. Consciousness comes after another step in the evolution of awareness, the step I have called "awareness *of.*" The sutra echoes this when it says, "The visible world, which is mind, does not exist [as seen by the senses], but mind is set in motion by being seen [i.e., objectified]."[23] The first part of this sentence—"the visible world, which is mind, does not exist [as seen by the senses]" — means the world is not something separate and apart. The second part of the sentence—"mind is set in motion by being seen"—is, in our terms, "awareness of awareness," or, in full, "awareness of awareness as the flower."

Let us now try to get a better understanding of "awareness of" by talking about the seventh level of consciousness, which is called manas. Suzuki says, "When this mind, which is designated in the sutra as the Alaya, is discriminated by an *erroneously self created and self reflecting agent called manas* [my italics], this world of particulars develops in its misleading fullness and richness."[24]

Pure awareness and "awareness as," although they form the background of our lives, are rarely encountered. In the same way, the light of the projector at a cinema, although it makes possible the whole film full of drama and color, rarely is noticed. Pure awareness and "awareness as," may seem to be abstract, remote, theoretical, and even questionable. Yet, many people have moments in their lives when either pure awareness or "awareness as" is no longer remote, but vivid, striking, giving a brief taste of sheer ecstasy or crumbling horror. So powerful are these flashes that people often divide their lives into before and after the experience. Abraham Maslow, a well-known psychologist of the 1960s, referred to these moments as peak experiences. In spiritual traditions they are called samadhi, enlightenment, near-death experiences, epiphany, and so on.

With manas and its consequences, by contrast, we move into a more familiar region, the region of "me" and "the world," the region of everyday experience of anxiety and joy, boredom and depression. It is not yet the region of identity, or "I," so is still upstream of full consciousness. Manas could be looked upon as a bridge between the different modalities of awareness and consciousness. It is also because of manas that individuality emerges. The sutra says, "Individualization is due to discrimination which is falsely interpreted and adhered to in a heart blinded by desires and passions, and, from this fact, there issue all kinds of human tragedies and comedies. What really exists is mind, which is above discrimination, that is, above logic and analysis."[25]

Here, an extremely important point must be made. It would appear that the sutra is simply putting forward a form of idealism or even solipsism. However, the "I" and "me" and "mine" are, as I am now going to show, themselves products of Alaya and manas working in conjunction. Alaya, therefore, is not a being, either individual or cosmic, and not a product of "my" consciousness, because "me," "my consciousness," and "the world," "God" all appear together at the same time.

The sutra says that memory (*vasana*), accumulating from the unknown past, makes discrimination possible. *Vasana* literally means "perfuming" or "fumigation": it is a kind of energy that is left behind when an action is accomplished that has the power to rekindle the old and seek out new impressions. This perfuming makes possible what is called reflection, or discrimination, and discrimination causes a world of opposites and contraries, with all their practical consequences, to emerge. This is why the sutra says, "The triple world is just the shadow of a self-reflecting and self-creating mind. Hence the doctrine of 'Mind' only." Although vasana makes discrimination possible, manas enables this possibility to be realized.

Manas

Manas is the seventh level of consciousness. A clear distinction between Alaya and manas cannot be made, just as we cannot make a clear distinction between the various levels of awareness: pure awareness, "awareness of," and "awareness as." This is because "manas is always depending on the Alaya, without which it has no reason of being in itself [but] the Alaya is also depending on manas. The Alaya is absolutely one, but this oneness gains significance only when it is realized by manas and recognized as its own supporter."[26]

Manas is Alaya in action through self-reflection; in Suzuki's words, "Alaya looks at itself in the mirror of manas."[27] As I pointed out, strictly speaking, manas is not a consciousness; it is the power by which consciousness is made possible. The sutra says that manas is "the active source of all the mental activities we ordinarily experience in this world of particulars. The *possibility* of consciousness lies in its dualistic nature, for without that which grasps and that which is grasped no conscious life is possible."[28]

The sutra also says that manas "is not only a discriminating intelligence, but a willing agency also."[29] Alaya has no active energy in itself. Earlier, I quoted Yasutani roshi saying that Alaya as ku is that which is living, dynamic; the sutra seems to be contradicting this. But we can now see that this contradiction is only apparent and is resolved through manas. Suzuki says the word *manas* includes in its meaning "to intend."[30] "The manas first wills, then it discriminates, and then judges; to judge is to divide, and this dividing ends in viewing existence dualistically. Hence the manas' tenacious attachment to the dualistic interpretation of existence. Willing and thinking are inextricably woven into the texture of manas."[31] We also could say that attention, too, is woven into the texture of manas. Attention enables us to judge and choose; it does this by focusing the dynamism of Alaya and making it active.

To sum up the distinctions, pure awareness differentiates within itself as "awareness as awareness" and "awareness as being." "Awareness as being" corresponds to the manifest aspect of Alaya. The next step in evolution is the emergence of "awareness of," which involves attention: we give attention to things, and this enables intention, willing, and judgment to emerge. None of these is a separate and distinct faculty or process, but all are different modes and degrees of "awareness of."

Manas, Manovijnana, and Language

With all this in mind, we now can see how, with the aid of what the sutra calls *manovijnana*, consciousness and the world evolve to create the impression "I am something in a world of somethings." As the sutra says, "In [its] activities manas is always found in company with Manovijnana . . . conjointly working to produce the world of particulars."[32] Manovijnana is the name given to the reasoning, logical, discriminating tendency. The function of manovijnana, Suzuki says, is "by hypothesis to reflect on manas as the eye vijnana reflects on the world of forms . . . but in fact, as soon as manas evolves the dualism of subject and object out of the absolute unity of the Alaya, then Manovijnana, and indeed all the other vijnanas, begin to operate."[33]

The sutra says manovijnana "has a field of its own as the perceiving of the rationality of things internal as well as external." This means that manovijnana is something like what we call the intellect: "It sometimes functions independently of the five senses and sometimes simultaneously and conjointly with them." In other words, it analyzes what we receive through the senses, or it simply acts on concepts, ideas, and thoughts. The sutra says, "It reflects on the duality, and from it issues a whole train of judgments with their consequent prejudices and attachments." This means that the dualisms of "me and the world," "me and you," "birth and death," "good and bad," "is and is not" arise out of manas but are fixed, by reflection and naming, by manovijnana. "In substance manas and Manovijnana are not different the one from the other, they depend upon the Alaya as cause and support." Manovijnana also has been known as "Manas in defilement."[34]

In *Outlines of Mahayana Buddhism*, Suzuki says that manovijnana is the "empirical ego." He says further that just as a silkworm imprisons itself in the cocoon it creates, manovijnana entangles itself in ignorance and takes its own illusory creations for realities.[35] The empirical ego is the belief "I am something," and this arises because the focal center, "me," is fixed by words. I use the word *fixed* here in the same way that one says one fixes a photograph. The effect of words is to provide, as it were, a buoy by which what otherwise would be a passing experience, lost in the sea of experience, is able to float and maintain the appearance of being permanent and constant. Lama Govinda interprets the *Lankavatara Sutra* as saying that manovijnana, which he calls the intellect, "conceives manas as the ego, because it is the apparently constant center of reference, in which the previous moment of consciousness is reflected."[36] In other words, manovijnana names the center of reference "I" and so gives it the appearance of permanence.

We come full circle with manovijnana. It is by the action of manovijnana that the world we know in everyday experience acquires the force of reality. It is therefore in manovijnana, and manas, that the turnabout known as kensho or satori must take place. What has hitherto been seen as having an objective reality must now be seen as being the mind itself. Instead of believing that I am aware of the room, I now see that I am aware of awareness as the room. As Suzuki says, "If it were the work of manas and Manovijnana that an external world came to be recognized as external, it must be their work again, properly executed this time, that we come to look upon the world as having evolved out of our own being." It could be said that the mind has hitherto been fixed on *something*, what Suzuki calls "the principle of particularization," and, thus, "the undesirable part of the Vasana or memory in the Alaya." "There must be," says Suzuki, "a turning of the waves, the course of manas and Manovijnana must be altered towards another direction than that which has been pursued hitherto." As Buddha says, "My Nirvana has nothing to do with Substance [what we have called "something"] nor with action, nor with appearance. With the cessation of the Vijnana which is caused by discrimination, there is my cessation." And "As when the great flood runs its course waves cease to rise, so with the extinction of [Manovijnana] all the vijnanas cease to arise."[37]

1. Daisetz T. Suzuki, *Studies in the Lankavatara* (Boulder: Prajna Press, 1978); *The Lankavatara Sutra*, translated by D. T. Suzuki (Boulder: Prajna Press, 1978), p. 44.

2. Suzuki, *Studies*, pp. 89, 101.

3. Ibid., p. xxxi.

4. Ibid., p. 89.

5. *Lankavatara Sutra*, p. 36.

6. Ibid., pp. 167, 169.

7. See Yasutani Hakuun, *Eight Points of Buddhism.*

8. *Lankavatara Sutra*, p. 49. The comments in brackets are provided by Suzuki.

9. Ibid., p. xxiii.

10. Ibid., p. 8.

11. Ibid., p. 25.

12. Ibid., p. xxiii.

13. Ibid., p. 67.

14. Philip Kapleau, ed., *The Three Pillars of Zen* (New York: Harper and Row, 1966), p. 74.

15. Suzuki, *Studies*, p. 176.

16. *Lankavatara Sutra*, p. 184.

17. Dogen, *The Time-Being*, translated by Dan Welch and Kazuaki Tanahashi, in *Moon in a Dewdrop*, edited by Kazuaki Tanahashi (New York: North Point Press, 1985), p. 78.

18. Suzuki, *Studies*, p. 167.

19. Ibid., p. 190.

20. Ibid.

21. See Albert Low, *The Butterfly's Dream* (Boston: Charles E. Tuttle, 1993), pp. xviii–xix. Ten people had to cross a river swollen by floods. The crossing was very precarious. When they got across they decided

to count their number to confirm all had made it. One of them stepped forward and counted. 1-2-3-4-5-6-7-8-9. There were only nine! Another stepped forward and counted—again, there were only nine. They were all bewailing the loss of one of their group when a stranger came along and asked them what the problem was. They said, "There were ten of us on the other side of the river and now, after a difficult crossing, there are only nine. We have lost one of our friends." The stranger said, "Let me count." So he counted, "1-2-3-4-5-6-7-8-9-10." They were so relieved that they continued their way rejoicing.

However, the stranger, too, was wrong. Can you see why? If you think there were really eleven when he counted, you, too, will be mistaken.

The mistake is that we always overlook the one who counts. If you overlook this one when you read the book, you will not be able to understand some parts. But, can you count the "tenth" person? If so how?

22. *Lankavatara Sutra*, p. xxii.

23. Suzuki, *Studies*, p. 175.

24. *Lankavatara Sutra*, p. 99.

25. Ibid.

26. Ibid., p. xxiv.

27. Ibid., p. xxv.

28. Ibid., p. 195 (my emphasis)

29. Suzuki, *Studies*, p. 191.

30. Ibid., p. 177.

31. *Lankavatara Sutra*, p. xxi.

32. Suzuki, *Studies*, p. 191.

33. Ibid., p. 191.

34. Ibid., p. 178, 191, 176.

35. D. T. Suzuki, *Outlines of Mahayana Buddhism* (New York: Schocken Books, 1963), p. 69.

36. Rider, Anagarika Govinda, *Foundations of Tibetan Mysticism* (London: 1960), p. 78.

37. Suzuki, *Studies*, pp. 200, 201, 193.

CHAPTER 7

THE *SURANGAMA SUTRA*

The moon's the same old moon
The flowers are just as they were
Yet now I am
The thingness of things.

Legend has it that the *Surangama Sutra* is the most important sutra because it will be the first to fall into extinction. With its demise, all the other sutras will follow into oblivion. Thus, some feel that the *Surangama Sutra* above all must be kept alive and flourishing. Nevertheless, according to D. T. Suzuki, no fewer than three Chinese versions of the sutra exist, and all three are different. I am using the text from *A Buddhist Bible* and have taken the liberty of modifying the language to make it more accessible to the general reader.

The Not-Seeing of the *Surangama Sutra*

The Hekiganroku has a koan based upon the *Surangama Sutra* which, in its way, points out one of its fundamental themes. I shall therefore use it as a way into the sutra. After discussing some aspects of the sutra, including some comments by a Zen master named Engo, we shall come back to the koan to see whether it appears any less opaque.

It is koan 94, and says, "In the *Surangama Sutra* the Buddha says, 'When I do not see, why do you not see my "not seeing?" If you see my "not seeing," naturally that is no longer "not seeing." If you do not see my "not seeing," it is naturally not a thing—how could it not be you?"'

Zen Master Engo, in some introductory words to the koan, says, "As to what stands prior to the Word, not one phrase has been handed down, even by the thousand holy ones. One thread maintains its continuity before your very eyes through countless eons. Entirely pure, entirely naked is the white ox under the blue sky. The golden-haired lion stands with eyes upturned, ears erect. Put the lion aside for the moment and tell me, what is the white ox under the blue sky?"

The white ox under the blue sky and the golden lion are the essence and function of Buddha nature—the first is often known as bodhi and the second as prajna. Engo refers to them as "what stands prior to the Word." Manjusri, the bodhisattva of wisdom, or of prajna, is sometimes shown seated on a lion. Whereas the Prajnaparamita sutras are concerned primarily with the golden lion, or prajna, the *Surangama Sutra* is concerned with the white ox, "entirely pure, entirely naked . . . under the blue sky."

The Senses and the One Mind

In particular, this sutra is about the six senses and their liberation. The sutra speaks of *six* senses because the discriminating mind is included among them. The senses are basically dependent upon what Engo called the white ox. Because they are all dependent upon bodhi, as pure knowing, they are basically of one nature, just as cheese, yogurt, and butter are all milk. However, they have become separated by ignorance into quasi-independent systems. Nevertheless, because they are of one nature, if one should be liberated—which means if one should return to its original nature as bodhi—all the others would be liberated also. One could say that they are like the leaves of a plant, all having the same stem as their source.

To quote the sutra, "Once we become aware that any particular sense perception, or even a thought based upon it, is unreal and fantastic, our dependence upon sense perceptions in general is overcome. After all the delusions of sense conceptions have been thus overcome, only the true Essence of mind will remain. This would mean that all the dusts of the world would be cleared by a single thought, and one would obtain the purity of perfect awakening."

This is the most important theme of the *Surangama Sutra*, a theme that was summed up succinctly by a Zen master who said, "If one sees through a speck of dust, one sees through the whole world."

To illustrate the relation of the six senses to the white ox, Buddha took a silk handkerchief and tied a knot in it. He then asked his disciples, "What is this?" They said that it was a knot. He tied another knot, asked the same question, and received the same answer. He continued in this way until he had tied six knots in the handkerchief. He then turned to Ananda and remarked, "When I showed you the first knot you called it a knot, and when I showed you the second, and third, and so on you still insisted that they were all knots."

Ananda replied, "The handkerchief itself is made of silk threads of different colors and woven into a single whole, one piece. But, when it is tied into a knot, it is correct to call it a knot. This would be true however many knots were tied in the handkerchief: they would all be knots. Why do you seem to be saying that only the first can be called a knot?"

Buddha then pointed out, "The silk handkerchief is one whole, one piece of woven silk. By my tying knots in it nothing has been changed except its appearance, even so it is still a handkerchief." This would seem to be a trivial point until we realize that we always forget that *the senses are simply ways of being of the One mind*. Gurdjieff used to say that we forget our*selves*, we do not remember ourselves. We are completely identified with what our senses give us. Above all, we are identified with the body because we are getting a stream of sensations from it all day. It is as well to remember the analogy of the mirror and reflections, although the analogy with the handkerchief is, in its way, much better. What we see, hear, taste, smell, and feel, as well as the kinesthetic sensations of the body, are all knots in the handkerchief, knots in the One mind. Zen Master Rinzai says much the same thing:

> Mind is without form and pervades the ten directions:
> In the eye it is called seeing,
> In the ear it is called hearing.
> In the nose it smells odors,
> In the mouth it holds converse.
> In the hands it grasps and seizes,
> In the feet it runs and carries.
> Fundamentally it is one pure radiance; divided it becomes the six harmoniously united spheres of sense. Since the mind is nonexistent, wherever you are, you are emancipated.

However, because we ignore the One mind, because we are identified with the senses and what they tell us, we are bound and in prison.

Buddha continued by asking, "If one were to take the sixth knot and start counting backwards, would the sixth knot then become the first?" Ananda said no, because when the handkerchief was tied six times, the last knot tied was the sixth. It cannot be called the first, because the order of the knots cannot be changed. The sixth knot is, and always will be, the sixth knot.

Although Ananda was right, Buddha went on to say, "The six knots may not all be the same, but, if you look for the *root* of their differences, you will find it in the fact that they are all arrangements of the one handkerchief." You cannot doubt the oneness of the handkerchief, although you can be doubtful about the knots: their differences, order, and so on. One cannot doubt the handkerchief because it is single and whole, so comparisons and opinions about it do not apply. The same is true of the six sense organs; they are knots tied in the essential unity of the mind.

Ananda agreed with this by saying that, as long as knots are tied in the handkerchief, one can discuss them and discriminate among them, question their order, and so on. When the knots are all untied, by contrast, no further discussion about them is possible because they are no more, and only the handkerchief remains. It is the same with the six senses and the one essence.

I used to give talks on management and, during the course of these talks, wanted to show people the importance of ideas. In order to do this I would hold up a piece of wood roughly cut into a wedge shape. I would then ask the group, "What is this? How much is it worth?" The natural response was "A piece of wood. It is worth nothing." I would continue to hold the wood up for a while and, sooner or later, someone would say, "A doorstop!" I would then pull from my pocket one of the rubber doorstops that one buys at the hardware store for a dollar or so and would ask, "What changed the worthless piece of wood into something of value?"

It is important to remember that when the doorstop appeared the piece of wood did not vanish, although it was now a doorstop and no longer a "piece of wood." An ancient Hindu saying puts it this way, "Stone, no dog; dog, no stone." Were one to look at a sculpture of a dog, one might well admire how well the sculptor had achieved the likeness of the dog, its canine quality, and so on. In this case one does not notice the stone. Or one could admire the stone; perhaps it is marble, so one could admire the veins, the shades of color, the smoothness, and so on. When one sees the dog, one does not see the stone; when one sees the stone, one does not see the dog.

As you sit in your room now, reading this book, if you look around for a moment, you will see the dog, not the stone; you will see the knots, not the handkerchief. The wall, the furniture, the window, the walls, ceiling, floor, the sounds, the pressure of the chair against your legs, your thoughts and your feelings—these, for most people, are all "the dog," they overlook "the stone." All that you see around you is as knots in the handkerchief—one knot is what you see, another is what you hear, another what you feel, and so on. The handkerchief is overlooked. But just as the piece of wood does not vanish when you see the doorstop, or the stone vanish when you see the dog, or the handkerchief vanish when you see the knots, so the One mind does not vanish when you see things and think thoughts. It could be said, though, that, when the world is real, I am a ghost; but, when I am real, the world is a dream.

Untying the Knots

Buddha then asked Ananda, "Suppose you preferred the original unity of the handkerchief without the knots, what would you do?" Ananda agreed that one would, of course, untie the knots, and he asked how this might be done. First of all Buddha tugged at the knots blindly, in a haphazard way; but this only pulled the knots tighter. After a while he turned to Ananda and asked, "I have tried now all ways to undo the knots, but without success. How would you untie them, Ananda?" Ananda replied, "I would first study the knot to find out how it was tied." One could say that the *Surangama Sutra*, and Zen practice, is, in part, a study of the knots so that they may be untied.

The Two Snares

Buddha goes on to point out that the knots cannot all be untied at once. The first knot that must be untied is the erroneous belief in an *I-personality*; the second is the belief in personal attainments and attributes of any kind. Zen Master Ta Hui said, "Go for the root; never mind about the branches, leaves, flowers, and fruit. Go for the root!" The root is the I-personality. Our whole life is devoted, at one level or another, to maintaining a sense of the self, which keeps in place the belief that I must be something. Buddha refers to this root when he speaks of two snares. Buddha is uncompromising. These two snares, he says—a belief in an I-personality and a belief in personal attainment—"must be utterly destroyed, and never again permitted to rise to defile the true Essential Mind."

The Secret Hiding Place of Mind

The key to this sutra lies in the questions Buddha then puts to Ananda: "What is it that gives the sensation of seeing? What is it that experiences this sensation? Who is it that experiences the feeling of pleasure of seeing?" These questions underlie all the koans. Often, when reading the koans one will come across a monk asking, "What is Buddha?" or "What is the meaning of Bodhidharma's coming from the West?" Or one will read of a master holding up a stick and demanding, "What is this?" These are all different ways of asking the same question: "What is it that everything comes out of? What is the source? What is the source of perception?" If one does not know where the perception of sight and the activities of the mind, originate, one will never be able to overcome one's worldly attachments and defilement.

Buddha refers to the sense of sight, but he wants this to stand for all sense perceptions, including the sixth sense, which we call the discriminating mind. He says it is like a king whose city was pestered by robbers and who tried to put an end to their thieving, but was unsuccessful because he could not locate their secret hiding place. Then Buddha asks Ananda the most basic of all questions on the spiritual way: "Do you know the secret hiding place of your eyes and mind?"

Ananda replies that earlier he had overheard Buddha explaining to some other disciples that the essence of the discerning mind (the secret hiding place) exists neither inside nor outside, nor between, in fact that it has no location of existence. And Buddha agrees, saying, "The essence of the discerning, perceptive, conscious mind has no definite location anywhere, it is neither in this world, in the vast open spaces, neither in water, nor on land, neither flying with wings, nor walking, nor anywhere."

This is reminiscent of a saying of Buddha that comes from one of the early sutras: "Beyond thought is that sphere wherein is neither earth nor water, fire nor air: it is not the infinity of space, nor the infinity of perception; it is not nothingness, nor is it neither idea nor non-idea; it is neither this world nor the next, nor is it both; it is neither the sun nor the moon. It neither comes nor goes, it neither abides nor passes away; it is not caused, established, begun, supported; it is the end of suffering."

A Zen master said the following about this same essence: "This pearl constantly moves around the five skandhas of each living being, showing itself and hiding itself, and its inward and outward radiance is of great supernatural power. Neither large nor small, it shines day and night, and illumines everything—yet when one looks for it, it is no thing and leaves no trace." A monk asked Zen Master Ummon what this "inward and outward radiance" was. Ummon shot back, "In what direction is your question pointed?" The questioner went on, "What does it mean to reach the light?" The master asked, "If someone suddenly asked you, what would you say?" The questioner persisted, "What about after reaching the light?" The master replied, "Forget the light, give me first the reaching!"

The entire *Surangama Sutra* is based upon the realization that freedom is possible through clarifying the secret source of the senses. Who is it that sees? Who is it that hears? Who is it that feels? By seeing into these questions it is possible to see into the secret place, or it might be better to say that one sees from what Engo called the white ox under the blue sky. The sutra says that to do this, for example, through the sense of hearing, one should "reverse one's outward perception of hearing and listen inwardly for the perfectly unified and intrinsic sound of your own Mind essence, and so attain to Supreme awakening." I have already referred several times to the koan "The Sound of One Hand Clapping," which asks, "You know the sound of two hands clapping; what is the sound of one hand clapping?" This koan points directly to this "intrinsic sound of your own Mind essence." When asking "Who am I?" one is undertaking the same search for the ground of knowing "I am." The question is not an invitation to find an identity for oneself, or to find "something" that one is, or to find "something" that knows. The white ox as bodhi is already knowing, it is already seeing and is already "I am." The light that Master Ummon referred to is already the reaching. All somethings, all identities, all experiences and sensations are but modifications of the white ox, knots in the handkerchief, eddies in the dynamic field of knowing.

Buddha said that, since beginningless time living beings have been led astray by believing that the nature of their mind is the same as the nature of an object. In this way, they lose their true and essential Mind; their minds are led astray by outer objects, and their seeing becomes subject to what is seen, and so is identified with outer conditions. "If one can learn to see things by one's true and essential Mind, then, right there and then, one will become equal to all the Tathâgatas. To do this we must carefully distinguish between the perception of objects and the intrinsic perception of sight by the Awakened Mind that is aware of the fallible perception through the eyes."

This, then, is the essential teaching of the *Surangama Sutra*:

We must realize that the True Nature of all our senses, of all our random perceptions and fleeting illusions, which become apparent when our senses are in the presence of objects, and which disappear when the objects are no longer present, *is* this mysterious, enlightening, intuitive essence. If we do not realize this, we cannot realize that all the phenomena of death and rebirth—their appearing, their activity, their disappearing—are simply the permanent, mysterious, enlightening, unchangeable, all perfect Wonderful Mind Essence of

Tathâgata's womb (wherein all is perfect purity, and unity and potentiality).

The questions "Who am I?" "What is Mu?" or "What is the sound of one hand clapping?" are ways to awaken to this Essence of mind. They are ways to let go of the belief that I am *something*, as well as the belief that the world is *something*, and, when I let go in this way, I realize the "mind essence."

In using this word *essence*, we see the treachery of words, because it suggests a substratum, a basis; it seems to be referring to the mirror to which the head monk referred in the *Platform Sutra*, and through which Hui Neng put his fist. Someone asked Joshu, possibly after having read the *Surangama Sutra*, "What is my mind essence?" Joshu said, "The tree sways, the bird flies about, the fish leaps, the water is muddy." If we talk about "essence" we commit the error of ignorance. Therefore, although throughout the sutra reference is made to the True Essence of Mind, saying that this underlies all perceptions, we must, when we read this, realize that neither the essence of the perception of sight nor any other essential nature transcending all objects has any objective existence. No such "thing," even the perception of sight, has any objective reality.

This may well cause confusion. Indeed, Ananda, in the sutra, complains that at one time Buddha says that the mind is tranquil, perfect, permanent, and essential in its nature, but he later says that, speaking truly, all expressions referring to Mind are nothing but figures of speech. How, then, queries Ananda, can it be said that even Buddha is an authentic teacher?

Buddha replies that we are confused by words: "This is like a man calling attention to the moon by pointing to it with his finger. The other man should look at the moon, but instead he looks at the finger. When he does this, he not only misses the moon, but misses the finger also. Why? Because he takes the finger for the moon, and confuses the shadows with light, because he confuses the shadow of the finger with the light of the moon."

Hearing Hearing

In the *Surangama Sutra,* Buddha and Ananda have an interesting conversation that can help us understand this point, as well as show us the way to True Essence of Mind that underlies all perceptions. I will report all of this conversation, because it is a very human interview, the kind that anyone could have with a teacher. Ananda first asks a question that must puzzle many: "If no mind exists, how are we to use it to get rid of false conceptions and attain the true?" In other words, how can we come to grips with this Mind that seems so elusive? How can we deal with it in a concrete way?

Buddha says, "To help you clear away these doubts I will ask you a few questions." He then strikes a gong and asks Ananda whether he hears the sound. Ananda replies yes. After the sound vibrations die away, Buddha asks, "Do you still hear?" Ananda says no, he no longer hears it. Buddha strikes the gong again and asks, "Did you hear the gong being struck?" Ananda says that he did. Buddha questions him, "Why do you reply at one time that you hear and at another time that you do not hear?" Ananda replies at once, "When the gong was struck I heard the sound, but when the vibrations died away, the sound ceased. That is what I meant when I said at one time that I heard, and at another time I did not hear."

Buddha tries again. He strikes the gong and inquires if Ananda can still hear. Ananda replies that he can. After a while the sound ceases, and Buddha asks again, "Do you still hear?" Ananda replies, a little impatiently this time, "No, the sound has stopped. How can I hear?"

Buddha says, "Ananda, what are you saying? At one time you say you hear, and at another you say you do not hear?" Ananda replies, possibly quite slowly this time, "Lord, when the gong is struck, there is sound; when the sound ceases there is no sound." "But," Buddha wants to know, "why do you make such confused statements?" Ananda retorts, "Lord, why do you accuse me of making confused statements? I only report the facts."

Buddha replies:

Why do I indeed? You do not seem to realize that the sound of the gong, the hearing of the sound, and the perception of the hearing are three different things, because you replied without seeming to recognize any difference. In fact a difference can be discerned between "sound" and "no sound" on the one hand, and "hearing" and "no hearing" on the other. Sound and no sound come and go, while hearing and no hearing are permanent. Sound and no sound are imaginary; hearing belongs to the pure Essence of Mind. Ananda, you are mistaken when you say that you no longer hear simply because there is no longer a sound. You heard the sound again when the gong was struck again, so it means that hearing was there all along.

This question that Buddha asks is a very famous one: "If the bell stops ringing, do you stop hearing?" Another variation on this theme is this question, which a master asked: "Does the sound go to the ear, or does the ear go to the sound?" When you hear a bird sing, it is evident that, as Buddha said, three things are involved: the first is the bird singing, that is the sound coming from the bird; the second is the ear that hears. But a third factor is also involved: knowing that the ear hears the bird singing. It is this third factor that is overlooked by most, even declared unnecessary by some. When the bird does not sing, the ear does not hear, *but hearing itself does not vanish.* Now, let me ask you, when you go to sleep, do you stop knowing?

Modern psychology is quite at home with the first two factors. But the third is ignored, denied, or explained as the result of the complexity of the organism, an epiphenomenon. Awareness, it is felt, arises in an organism when the nervous system reaches a certain degree of sophistication, and most scientists are convinced that, in time, they will be able to explain consciousness completely by reference to the wiring of the brain. In other words, they would do away with the third factor entirely. Yet it is this third factor, the white ox, which Buddha is saying is fundamental.

As Buddha points out, hearing belongs to the essence of Mind; if one remembers this, one will not seem to hear at one time and not to hear at another. By means of the illustration with the bell, he says, we must see that, in spite of the destruction of our bodies, and the gradual exhaustion of the vitality of our life, the essential nature of the hearing is neither destroyed nor caused to vanish. Buddha is tackling, among other things, the ever-present human fear of death and impermanency. We fear that we may, after all, be nothing, that, when the bell stops ringing, we will stop hearing. We ask, fearfully, "When the senses, at death, are no longer active, will I stop knowing and vanish into nonexistence?"

"If you could only learn from this," Buddha goes on,

and so become free from your bondage to death and rebirth, and from your fear of impermanency, if you could learn to concentrate your mind on its true and permanent nature, then the eternal light would illumine you. This, in turn, would mean that all the particular and discriminated perceptions of things, sense organs, false imaginings, self and not self, would be seen as illusions, because the phenomena of the thinking mind are only empty, and the transitory things as well as the various emotions of your mortal consciousness are simply passing phenomena. If you can learn to ignore these two fundamental illusions—death and rebirth and the fear of impermanence—and hold fast to the Immutability known by the Eye of Dharma, then you will have no fear of not attaining Supreme Awakening.

In view of this statement, you might ask yourself: When I no longer think a thought, where does it go? Our whole life is suspended on the thread of thought, idea, conception. When the thought stops thinking, does knowing stop knowing?

Awakening

The sutra says that two fundamental principles—ignorance and compassion—must be realized if one wishes to come to awakening.

Ignorance

The principle of ignorance makes us look for what the sutra calls "the outgoing principle of individuation." I have addressed this topic in other writings, pointing out that we all try to be unique in the world, we all try to be special, superior, and this effort leads us to separate ourselves from others and so suffer all the ills that follow. The separation of "me" from "you," "me" from "the world" is the outgoing principle of individuation.

It is through ignorance, also, that we want to feel we are in control of situations, and this desire causes us to judge and discriminate constantly, and because of this judging and discriminating we mistake the empirical, confused, and defiled mind for the true and natural Essence of Mind. As Buddha said, from the beginning of time down to the present life, we have been constantly misunderstanding our true nature and essential Mind. It is like treating a petty thief as my own son. He then says categorically, "Your being is not your discriminating mind!"

He asks, "Why do you so persistently permit your thoughts to rise and fall, letting the body rule the Mind, instead of the Mind ruling the body? Why do you let your senses deceive you as to the true unchanging nature of Mind, and see things in a reversed order? This leads to agitation and confusion and suffering. As one forgets the true nature of Mind, so one mistakes the reflections of objects for one's own Mind." He also declares, "All of you have been accepting this confusing conception of phenomena as being your own mind. As long as you accept it as your true mind, is it any wonder that you become bewildered and suppose it to be localized in your physical body, and suppose further that all the external things—mountains, rivers, the great open spaces, and the whole world—were outside the mind? Is it any wonder that you failed to realize that everything you have so far falsely conceived exists only within your own wonderful enlightening mind of True Essence?"

Compassion

The second fundamental principle is the principle of compassion, which draws together rather than separates. It is a unifying principle of purity, harmony, likeness, rhythm, permanency, and peace. Whereas the principle of ignorance is outgoing, this principle is indrawing and, to quote the sutra, "By the indrawing of this principle within the light of your own nature, its unifying spirit can be discovered and developed and realized under all varieties of conditions."

Buddha then issues the following challenge: "Ananda, I challenge you, by the perception of your sight, to detect which is my True essence and which manifestation. The massing clouds, the flying birds, the hurrying winds, the rising of dust, the mountains, the familiar woods, trees, rivers, herbs, vegetables, animals, none of them belongs to my True nature." It is this discernment of what is the mirror apart from the reflections, what is knowing apart from that which is known, that is the challenge of zazen.

This challenge leads into the conversation that contributes to the koan in the *Hekiganroku*, quoted at the beginning of the chapter. Ananda asks, "Regarding all these things, far and near, as perceived by the pure Essence of your perceiving eyes, they have different characteristics, but the perception of our eyes is always the same. Does this mean that this wonderful perception, this seeing, is the true nature of our minds?"

Buddha replies,

If seeing is not your own nature but, instead, could be considered to be *something*, then, because it is considered to be something, my seeing would have to be considered to be something as well. Because my seeing is then something, it would mean that you should be able to see my seeing. Moreover, if you see the same thing as I do, and believe that because of this you are seeing my seeing, then because you have seen the sphere of my seeing, you should see my "not seeing" also. Why can't you do so? Furthermore, if you say that you see my "not seeing," this would not be true, because then it would simply be your own "not seeing" and could not be my "not seeing." If this is so, how can your "not seeing" be regarded as mine? Therefore, if you really do not see my "not seeing," then the essence of this "not seeing" cannot be an object that can be seen with the eyes and touched with the hands. If it is not an object, then is it not your true nature? If you still persist in considering your seeing as an object, then the object should be able to see you too. If you try to explain seeing as an object in this way, the objectivity of an object and the selfness of seeing the object would be hopelessly jumbled together. No one would be able tell which is subject and which is object.

We take it for granted that we share a common world. I believe that what I see, you see also. If something can be seen, then it seems to be obvious that we both can see it. Mingled with this assumption is the additional belief that my *seeing* something is the same as your *seeing* that something. It is this tacit assumption that has underlain the myth of scientific objectivity. According to this myth, not only is the world a shared world, but our vision of the world is a shared vision. It is, of course, recognized that prejudices and biases overlay this shared vision and influence what each of us sees; it is recognized, also, that language, as a filter, conditions how we see things. Nevertheless, it is assumed without question that we all share a common world and a common seeing of that world.

This assumption has an additional implication: If I should not be alive to see the world, then you would continue to see the world for me. A person concerned that her memory should live on after her death sees, in her mind's eye, future generations seeing the world, somewhat modified by the dead person's memory, but also seeing the world *for* the dead person. All these beliefs underlie this sentence in the sutra: "You see the same thing as I do, and believe that because of this you are seeing my seeing."

However, the sentence in full says, "*If* you see the same thing as I do, and believe that because of this you are seeing my seeing, then because you have seen the sphere of my seeing, you should see my 'not seeing' also." In other words, the *Surangama Sutra* is challenging the most basic assumptions that everyone takes for granted: that a common world exists, and that we have a shared vision of that world. I just said that everyone takes these for granted, although in modern theoretical physics it now is recognized that the observer is an intrinsic part of the observation, something that the *Surangama Sutra* is saying in the section we are dealing with now.

This brings us back to the koan at the beginning of this chapter, "When I do not see, why do you not see my 'not seeing'? If you see my 'not seeing,' naturally that is no longer 'not seeing.' If you do not see my 'not seeing,' it is naturally not a thing—how could it not be you?"

Let us explore the "not seeing." Buddha asks, "Why can you not see my 'not seeing'?" In this question the expression "not seeing" is used in two quite different ways. Buddha refers to Ananda's not-seeing and to his own not-seeing. He says that Ananda cannot see Buddha's not-seeing; in other words, Ananda's not-seeing is a lack, a kind of failure. But Buddha's not-seeing is not a lack, quite the contrary. In the first koan of the *Hekiganroku*, Emperor Wu asks Bodhidharma, "Who are you?" And Bodhidharma answers, "I don't know." In fact, the correct translation from the Chinese of the emperor's reply would be "Not-knowing." The "I don't know" is bowing to the demands of language and good style. After Bodhidharma has left, the courtier asks the emperor, "Do you know who that man was, my lord?" and the emperor replies, "I don't know! [not-knowing]." One of the points of the koan is to distinguish between these two not-knowings. The second, the emperor's, is a lack, a failure. But Bodhidharma's is not. The not-knowing of Bodhidharma and the not-seeing of Buddha are pointing in the same direction. But what are they pointing to? In Buddha's illustration of ringing a bell, when the bell stops ringing, "not hearing" takes over. But this is not an absence, or a failure, any more than Bodhidharma's not-knowing, or Buddha's not-seeing, is a failure or a lack.

In Buddhism, several forms of blindness are mentioned. Physical blindness means a person's eyes are defective. But a person can be so prejudiced that he does not see. This is another kind of blindness. When someone comes to awakening, she is very often overtaken by the new way of seeing. This, too, is a kind of blindness, the blindness of emptiness. But then Buddha is blind; this is the blindness of "not seeing."

Each of us is *a* world; we are not part of *the* world. We do not share a world, nor do we share seeing the world. Buddha said on another occasion, "Throughout heaven and earth I alone am the Honored One." When he said that, he was speaking for all of us. When he says, "I alone am the Honored One," he is speaking from "not knowing, not seeing." To say, "I *alone* am the Honored One" does not mean that we are beings totally isolated one from the other. The *Hwa Yen Sutra* states that all worlds interpenetrate without obstruction, which means that, far from being isolated, we are the other as well as ourselves. I am you, as well as me. This is brought home in koan 94 because when it says, "How could it not be you?" Zen Master Setcho adds the comment, "To say you or me is totally beside the point." In other words, Buddha could equally well have said, "If you do not see my 'not seeing', how could it not be me?" "You" and "me" are two halves of One world; both are essential, and both in their ways are the whole. To see into the One world is wisdom. To see into the two halves is compassion.

Let us return to Ananda's "not seeing" and Buddha's "not seeing." We could say that Ananda's "not seeing" is the not-seeing of the personality, whereas Buddha's "not seeing" is the not-seeing of True nature, it is the not-seeing of the white ox. It is because of Buddha's not-seeing that Ananda's not-seeing as well as his seeing are possible. We cannot see Buddha's not-seeing. Putting this in terms of practice, when we ask, "Who am I?" we do not eventually get an answer and so come to awakening. In other words, we go not from a not-knowing to a knowing but from one kind of not-knowing to another.

The first is a not-knowing for lack of information, or because one has the wrong information. It is the not-knowing of ignorance. The other kind of not-knowing is *absence of content*. If the bell stops ringing, do you stop hearing, or are you still hearing but there is no content to the hearing? When thinking stops thinking, does knowing stop knowing? When the monk asked Joshu whether a dog has Buddha nature and Joshu answered, "Mu!" "No!" this was not a no of denial, but a no such as in Hui Neng's "From the beginning not a thing exists," or Hakuin's "True self is no self." It is the no of the *Prajnaparamita*: no eyes, ears, nose, tongue, body, mind. It is the "not" of not-hearing, not-seeing.

Returning to the koan, it says, "If you do not see my 'not seeing,' it is naturally not a thing—*how could it not be you?*" How could my "not seeing" not be you? The sutra elaborates, "If you really do not see my not seeing, then the selfness of this not seeing cannot be an object that can be seen with the eyes and touched with the hands. And if it is not an object, then why is it not your true nature?"

Buddha talks of "the selfness of the not seeing." What does this mean? When we practice, we are constantly told to practice from *within*. Unfortunately, many people think this means within their body, or their mind, or their feelings. Many close their eyes when practicing, thinking that they can go further within by not being distracted by sights, sounds, and so on from without. However, to practice from within means to see that nothing lies outside. Practice from within means practice that is purely subjective. Most of us understand the word *subjective* to mean the opposite of *objective*. To be "too subjective" means to interpret things too much from the standpoint of one's own likes and dislikes, from one's own point of view. But there is another meaning of *subjective*: not divided into inside and outside, without separation. *Subjective* and *within* are, then, synonyms.

The Verse

The koan in the *Hekiganroku* has a verse by Zen Master Setcho that says:

> *"The whole Elephant" or the "whole Ox" both blinding*
> *cataracts*
> *The wisest have groped in the dark.*
> *Do you want to see the golden-haired Buddha?*
> *Through countless eons, none is more than halfway there.*

Who does not know the story of the blind men investigating the elephant? One grabbed its ear and said that the elephant was a big leaf; another grasped its leg and said, "No, it is a tree trunk!" Another felt its belly and said that it was a huge barrel. Another caught hold of its tail and said that it was a long piece of rope. A man who could see came by laughing, because he could see the whole elephant. But, as Setcho says, he was the blindest of all. Whether we talk of the whole elephant, the white ox, Buddha nature, or the Essence of Mind, they are all blinding cataracts.

"The wisest have groped in the dark." We may have read the sutras diligently, learned all the names, and understood all the references, but all of this is but pouring from the empty in the void, groping in the dark.

Setcho asks, "Do you want to see the golden-haired Buddha?" Well, do you, and if you do, how will you see him? The alchemists say, "Our sun is a black sun!" Zen Master Tokusan came to awakening after his teacher had put out the light.

"Through countless eons, none is more than halfway there." A monk was asked whether he agreed with what his teacher said. He replied, "I agree with half." The questioner went on, "Why don't you agree with it all?" "I would not be doing justice to my teacher," he said. The world of reflections is a whole world. The world of the mirror is a whole world. But each is only half.

GLOSSARY

People

Chinese Zen Masters

Bodhidharma (Chinese, P'u-t'I-ta-mo, 470–543) Bodhidharma was the first Chinese patriarch of Zen and of the martial arts. His temple at Shao-lin now is a center of pilgrimage for those practicing the martial arts. He is the subject of the first koan of the *Hekiganroku* and of koan 41 of the *Mumonkan*.

Doshin (Chinese, Tao-hsin, 580–651) The fourth Zen patriarch and an ardent devotee of Zen, Doshin also taught his students the *Lankavatara Sutra*.

E'no (Chinese, Hui Neng, 638–713) The sixth and last Zen patriarch, E'no is one of the best-known and revered Zen masters. It is said that with his teaching Zen finally let go of its Indian coloration and became truly Chinese. E'no is the subject of koans 23 and 29 of the *Hekiganroku*.

Engo (Chinese, Yuan-wu K'o-ch'in, 1063–1135) Engo provided introductions and commentaries to the koans in the *Hekiganroku*.

Ganto (Chinese, Yen-t'ou Chuan-huo, 828–887) Ganto lived during a very turbulent period and was stabbed to death by some robbers who had invaded his temple. It is said that his cry could be heard for miles around. Hakuin could not understand how a Zen master could cry out so at his death. This perplexity was resolved at the time of Hakuin's awakening, when he cried out, "I am Ganto!" Ganto was the subject of koan 13 in the *Mumonkan* and of koans 51 and 66 of the *Hekiganroku*.

Hogen (Chinese, Fa Yen, 885–958) A student of the *Avatamsaka Sutra*, Hogen is the subject of koan 26 in the *Mumonkan*.

Hui K'o (487–593) Koan 41 of the *Mumonkan* says that Hui K'o, the second Chinese patriarch, was so desperate for Bodhidharma's teaching that he stood in deep snow for a long time and eventually cut off his right arm to show his sincerity.

Hyakujo (Chinese, Pai-chang, Huai-hai, 720–814) One of the most famous of the Chinese Ch'an masters of the T'ang dynasty. A student and successor to Ma-tsu Tao-i, he founded the Ch'an monastic tradition.

Joshu (Chinese, Chao-chou Ts'ung-shen, 778–897) One of the most important Zen masters of China, Joshu was a student and dharma heir of Nansen. He came to awakening at the age of eighteen and stayed with Nansen until the latter died when Joshu was about sixty. After that he went on pilgrimage until he was eighty and only then started to teach in a formal way. He died when he was 119 years old. He is the subject of koans 1, 7, 11, 14, 19, 31, and 37 of the *Mumonkan* and 2, 9, 30, 41, 45, 52, 57, 58, 59, 64, 80, and 96 of the *Hekiganroku*.

Mumon (Chinese, Wu-men Hui-k'ai, 1183–1260) The compiler of the *Mumonkan*, Mumon was one of the greatest Rinzai Zen masters of his day. It is said that he worked for eight years on the koan "Mu!" and then one day, when the drum was struck to indicate midday, he came to awakening. His awakening verse was "Out of the clear sky with the sun shining brightly, suddenly a thunderclap."

Nansen (Chinese, Nan-ch'uan P'u-yuan, 748–835) The student and
dharma successor of Ma-Tsu, Nansen had seventeen dharma
successors, the greatest of whom was Joshu. He is the subject
of many koans including 14, 19, 27, and 34 of the *Mumonkan*
and 28, 31, 40, 63, 64, and 69 of the *Hekiganroku*.

Rinzai (Chinese, Lin-chi I-hsuan, d. 866) A student of the great Zen
master Huang P'o, Rinzai founded the school that was named
after him. He is best known for the vigor of his teachings,
which included shouts and blows from his stick. He is the subject of koans 20 and 39 of the *Hekiganroku*.

Tokusan (Chinese, Te-shan Hsuan-chien, 781–867) Tokusan originally was a teacher of the *Diamond Sutra*. When he heard that
the Zen sect was teaching the possibility of becoming Buddha
in one lifetime, he went to refute their claims and was awakened by Ryotan. He is the subject of koans 13 and 28 of
the *Mumonkan* and koan 4 of the *Hekiganroku*. He was the
teacher of Ganto.

Japanese Zen Masters

Bassui (1327–1387) Bassui was an outstanding Japanese Zen master
of the Rinzai tradition.

Dogen (1200–1253) The greatest of the Zen masters, Dogen came
to deep awakening in China. Although he taught the Soto
method of Zen and emphasized the importance of shikantaza,
or just sitting, he also used koan practice. He made a collection of over 300 koans, adding his own commentaries.

Hakuin Zenji (1689–1769) The father of modern koan practice,
Hakuin revived this practice at a time when it was almost
extinct. He introduced the koan "The Sound of One Hand
Clapping." He was deeply enlightened, having had numerous
great and small kenshos.

Hakuun Ryoko Yasutani (1885–1973) One of the first authentic Zen
masters to teach in the West, Yasutani roshi started his Zen

training in the Soto Zen tradition, then turned to the Rinzai and Soto teaching of his teacher Harada roshi.

Shenryu Suzuki (1905–1971) Founder of the Zen Center in San Francisco and author of *Zen Mind, Beginners' Mind*.

Tibetan Zen Masters

Milarepa (1025–1135) The most famous of Tibet's holy men.

Buddha's Disciples

Ananda Buddha's cousin and personal attendant. It was due to Ananda's prodigious memory that the early, Theravadin sutras, came into existence. It is said that after Buddha's death he remembered Buddha's teachings word for word and dictated them to be written down. In spite of, or perhaps because of, his great intellectual powers, Ananda was unable to come to awakening until after Buddha's death. Koan 22 of the *Mumonkan* describes his awakening.

Avalokita Although one of Buddha's disciples, Avalokita also became one of the three important bodhisattvas of the Mahayana School, the bodhisattva of compassion. The other two are Manjusri and Samanthabhadra. It is said that Avalokita, who is known as Kuan Yin in China and Kannon in Japan, has a thousand eyes to see the suffering of the world and a thousand arms to help.

Manjusri Also a disciple of Buddha, as the bodhisattva of wisdom, Manjusri is one of the three principal bodhisattvas of the Mahayana School.

Maudgalyana. Maudgalyana was one of Buddha's chief disciples.

Sariputra Another of Buddha's chief disciples, Sariputra was considered by Buddha to be the foremost of the wise.

Subhuti A bodhisattva particularly important in the Prajnaparamita tradition, Subhuti was famous for his contemplation of emptiness. He appears in the *Diamond Sutra*.

Upali A disciple of Buddha, Upali is noted for his mastery of the Vinaya tradition. He appears in the *Vimalakirti Sutra.*

Others

Amida Buddha The Buddha of boundless light, Amida Buddha is particularly beloved by followers of the Pure Land School, a devotional school of Buddhism.

Desert Fathers Christian hermits of the fourth century A.D. who fled Alexandria looking for salvation in the desert.

Nisargadatta Maharaj A deeply awakened Hindu who died in 1982, Nisargadatta had his conversations recorded in the book *I Am That.* At the age of thirty-five, he met a teacher, and within three years he had awakened to his true nature.

Ramana Maharshi A deeply awakened modern Hindu sage, Ramana died in 1950. At the age of seventeen he had a terrible fear of death, but he decided to accept whatever was about to happen and came to deep awakening as a consequence. His conversations have been recorded.

Sri Aurobindo (1872–1950) A modern Hindu teacher, Sri Aurobindo was the founder of Integral Yoga.

St. John of the Cross (1542–1591) St. John is one of the most highly regarded Christian mystics. Part of a movement to reform the monastic life of his time, he was incarcerated in the Carmelite monastery of Toledo in a cell so small that he was unable to stand upright. It was in these terrible conditions that he came to deep awakening. His book *The Dark Night of the Soul* is a classic throughout the Christian world.

St. Julian of Norwich An anchoress of the 14th century who had many "showings" or revelations of God's love in a series of visions which she wrote about, and commented upon, in her book *Showings.*

St. Teresa of Avila (1515–1582) One of the most famous Christian mystics, St. Teresa was responsible for opening a number of convents in Spain. St. John of the Cross was her mentor and confessor. Her autobiography, *The Interior Castle*, is a classic of Christian mysticism.

St. Thérèse of Lisieux (1873–1897) A more recent mystic, the French St. Thérèse died young of tuberculosis. The book *St. Thérèse of Lisieux: Her Last Conversations* has been an inspiration for many people following a spiritual practice.

Terms and Titles

alchemy The process by which lead, or the *massa confusa*, is turned to gold. In spiritual practice, the lead, or confused mass, is the collection of negative emotions, anguish, and suffering that make up the personality.

anatman "No I"; *muga* in Japanese.

anicca "No thing."

apophatic From a Greek word meaning "denial," a spiritual way also known as the via negativa. God is said to have no characteristics or qualities other than He is.

arhat Literally "worthy one," one for whom the present life is the last; after it he will have attained complete purity and Nirvana.

Atman According to the Vendanta tradition of Hinduism, the real, immortal self of a person.

Bhagavad Gita The song of God, a long, ancient Indian poem purporting to be a conversation between Arjuna, a warrior, and Krishna in which the virtues of a spiritual life, particularly one lived fully in the world, are extolled. The *Bhagavad Gita* forms part of a much longer epic called the *Mahabharata*.

Bodhi Knowing without reflection.

Bodhisattva One who seeks awakening through the practice of the virtues of *paramitas*, but who renounces entry into complete Nirvana until all beings have been saved.

Bompu Zen Zen that is free from philosophical or religious content and is practiced for physical and mental health.

The Cloud of Unknowing A mystical text written by an anonymous author in the 14th century. The teaching given in this book has many similarities with the teaching of Zen Buddhism.

dharani Short sutras composed of syllables of symbolic meaning.

dharmas Phenomena; all that has form.

dhyana Steadfastness of mind that leads to samadhi.

Dukkha Suffering; literally *du* (two) *kha* (ness).

haiku Seventeen-syllable poems that have been very popular in Japan.

Hekiganroku (Chinese, *Pi Yen Lu*) A collection of a hundred koans compiled by Zen Master Setcho, who appended a verse to each koan. Most of the koans are preceded by an introduction by Zen Master Engo, who also commented on each koan.

Joriki Energy of concentration.

karma A sanskrit word which literally means "deed." It is used to refer to the collection of intentions and deeds committed in the past which have influence in the present.

kataphatic From a Greek word meaning "affirmation," the way that ascribes to God all the positive virtues.

klesa Literally defilement, trouble, passion. Klesa is that action which causes suffering to others and to oneself. The three principal klesa are: ignorance, hatred, and greed.

ku The "substance" of the Buddha nature. Ku is not merely emptiness, but is that which is living, dynamic, devoid of mass, beyond all individuality, and the matrix of all phenomena.

Mahasattva Maha means great, and *sattva* means being.

Mahayana Literally *maha* (great) *yana* (vehicle).

mantra Literally "protection of the mind." A mantra is a single word or short phrase repeated for different reasons depending on the level of aspiration of the student and the level of competence of the teacher.

mondo question and answer, usually between a monk and his master.

Mu! Literally "No!" The first koan in the *Mumonkan*. To see into Mu! is to see into one's own true nature.

muga Japanese for "no I."

Mumonkan A collection of forty-eight koans compiled by Zen Master Mumon. Each koan has a commentary and verse by Mumon.

Nirvriti A condition of blessed rest sought by those practicing the Hinayana way.

ox Symbol of the true self. The ox is used in a series of images indicating the steps or stages from initial awakening through search to full enlightenment.

paramitas That which has reached the other shore; transcendence.

personality A collection of memories, ideas, judgments, and values around a focal point called "I."

prajna Aroused mind, knowing freed from the sheaths of knowledge.

Prajnaparamita A school of Buddhism that seeks liberation through recovery of pure knowing. This school has some forty sutras, most composed at the beginning of the Common Era, as the basis of its teaching.

Pure Land A Buddha realm. As there are countless Buddhas, there are countless Buddha realms. However, the Pure Land School of the Mahayana, which is based on the *Lotus Sutra*, looks upon the Pure Land of the West as the principal Buddha realm. This realm is presided over by Amida (Amitabha in Sanskrit) Buddha.

samadhi A condition in which subject and object are no longer evident, so mental activity is brought to rest. There are many levels of samadhi, some with content and some without; the highest level is that within which all life unfolds.

Samsara Literally "journeying." Samsara is everyday life, the constant round of birth and death.

sattva Being - it is derived from "sat" which means "eternal being"

shikantaza Literally *shikan* (nothing but) *ta* (precisely) *za* (sitting), just sitting. In shikantaza practice one sits in the faith that one is whole and complete. In the Rinzai School shikantaza normally is assigned only after a person has completed the koan practice.

skandhas Literally "heap," "group," or "collection." The skandhas are the personality made up of five elements: form, emotion, thought, will, and consciousness.

Theravada Teaching of the Elders. Theravada, the earliest form of Buddhism, generally differentiated from Mahayana, principally is followed in Southeast Asia.

vasanas Submerged and hidden desires and ambitions that can erupt at any given moment.

Vedanta Literally *veda* (knowledge) and *anta* (end). Therefore, *Vedanta* means the conclusion of the Vedas as contained in the Upanishads.

Weltanschauung A German word meaning "world idea" or "world-view."

wu-wei An action that is to the point but is not brought about by intention.

zazen Literally "sitting Zen." *Zen* is a Japanese word based on the Chinese ideogram *ch'an*, which in turn is an alliteration of the Sanskrit word *dhyana*.

BIBLIOGRAPHY

Prajnaparamita Hridaya

The Sutra

The Prajnaparamita Hrydaya Taken from Daily Chants and Cere-monies, Rochester, NY: The Rochester Zen Center, 1975.

Commentary

Ch'an and Zen Teaching. Edited and translated by Ku K'uan Yu. [Charels Luk] London: Rider and Co., 1960.

Conze, Edward. *Buddhist Studies, 1934–72*. Oxford: Bruno Cassier, 1967.

———. *Buddhist Wisdom Books*, London: Unwin, 1978.

Lopez, Donald, S., Jr. *The Heart Sutra Explained*. Albany: State University of New York Press, 1988.

Diamond Sutra

The Sutra

Blythe, R. H. *Selections from the Diamond Sutra Taken from Zen and*

Zen Classics, vol. 4, *The Mumonkan*. Tokyo: Hokuseido Press, 1966.

The Diamond Sutra. London: Concord Grove Press, 1983.

The Diamond Sutra and The Sutra of Hui Neng. Translated by A. F. Price and Wong Mou-Lam. Clear Light Series. Berkeley: Shambhala, 1969.

Commentary

Ch'an and Zen Teaching. Edited and translated by Ku Ku'an Yu. London: Rider and Co., 1960.

Vimalakirti Sutra

The Sutra

The Holy Teaching of Vimalakirti. Translated by Robert Thurman. University Park and London: Pennsylvania State University Press, 1976.

The Vimalakirti Nirdesa Sutra. Translated and edited by Charles Luk. Berkeley: Shambhala, 1972.

Lankavatara Sutra

The Sutra

The Lankavatara Sutra. Translated by D. T. Suzuki. Boulder: Prajna Press, 1978.

Self Realization of Noble Wisdom (The Lankavatara Sutra). Compiled by Dwight Goddard. Clearlake, CA: Dawn Horse Press, 1983.

Commentary

Suzuki, Daisetz T. *Studies in the Lankavatara*. Boulder: Prajna Press, 1978.

Surangama Sutra

The Sutra

"The Surangama Sutra." In *A Buddhist Bible*. Edited by Dwight Goddard. Boston: Beacon Press, 1966.

The Koans

Hekiganroku

The Bluecliff Record. Translated by J. C. Cleary. Boulder: Prajna Press, 1977.

Mumonkan

Low, Albert. *The World: A Gateway: Commentaries on the Mumonkan*. Boston: Charles E. Tuttle, 1995.